OPERATING
A BOOKSTORE

OPERATING A BOOKSTORE

Practical Details for Improving Profit

by Eliot Leonard

BOOKSELLERS PUBLISHING, INC.

*A Wholly Owned Subsidiary of
the American Booksellers Association*

BOOKSELLERS PUBLISHING, INC.

A wholly owned subsidiary of the American Booksellers Association
828 South Broadway
Tarrytown, NY 10591
(914) 591-2665, (800) 637-0037

Cover design: Joan Adelson

ISBN: 1-879923-04-1

First Printing, May 1992

Second Printing, February 1994

Printed in the United States of America

Contents

About the Author

E liot Leonard grew up in Boston, and at the age of ten he began working in his family's clothing stores, where he learned the basics of retailing. He received a degree in Business Administration from Boston University in 1936. In September of that year, he was offered a two-week job at the Harvard Coop in Cambridge. That two-week stint turned into a 29-year stay. In 1965, Leonard accepted an executive position with Pickwick Bookshop in Hollywood, California. In 1968, the Pickwick stores were acquired by the Dayton Hudson Corporation, and in 1972, when Pickwick merged with B. Dalton Bookseller, Leonard was named senior vice president and stores director of the western region. He retired in 1980.

Leonard was active in the bookselling community for many years. He was a member of the board of directors of the American Booksellers Association and served a two-year term as ABA president. He also chaired numerous National Association of College Stores committees. Leonard has written articles for *College Store, Publishers Weekly,* and *American Bookseller.* An instructor at dozens of ABA Booksellers Schools, Leonard always took special pleasure in helping new bookstores. At the 1987 ABA Convention in Washington, DC, Leonard was honored "for His 50 Years in Bookselling and His Contributions to the Education of His Fellow Booksellers."

Introduction

I n my forty years of active bookselling plus ten years of bookstore consultation work, many people have asked me about the secret of bookselling success. Unfortunately, there is no single answer.

I was a neophyte when I fell into bookselling by chance in 1936, as a temporary clerk in the trade book department of a large college store. I knew retailing fairly well, having been brought up working in the family's clothing store, but I had no background in literature or bookselling. I wasn't aware that many titles are issued in more than one edition, that almost all hardcover books come with dust jackets, and I had not heard of terms such as reprints, bestsellers, *Publishers Weekly*, ABA, Everyman's Library, and hundreds of others. There were many embarrassing moments in those early days, when customers would inquire about a classic and I would ask if it was a newly published title. I gradually learned about the contents of books, and about authors and titles—enough to buy and merchandise them for many years.

People become booksellers for a variety of reasons. Many have a book background—some work in libraries, some are teachers, others are browsers who greatly enjoy the time they spend in bookstores. Some prospective booksellers have a sizable collection of books at home and wish to try their hand at running a bookshop. Over the last decade, however, an increasing number of people come to bookselling from other fields, often starting a second career in mid-life. The entrepreneurs of the 1980s have found bookselling.

Having discussed the book trade with hundreds of would-be booksellers, I have discovered that, regardless of their background, most have wrong assumptions about the ease and profitability of the book business. It's true that bookselling is an exhilarating profession. Looking in from the outside, the would-be bookseller might think it a clean, easy-to-run kind of store, and one that is very profitable. But it is not the gentle profession it seems to be, nor once was. When you are inside, involved in the day-to-day operation, the romance of the book often disappears. There you are, working minute by minute, day after day, stocking, handling, and selling. Opening packages, marking books, cleaning shelves, and ringing the register are part of the daily routine, just as it is in other kinds of stores. You are not spending the day reading books.

I remember reading a few years ago that among fifty categories of stores, and departments in stores, books were near the bottom of the list for profitability and return on investment, and I have not found evidence of change in recent years. Because of the detail involved in handling books, work hours required are appreciably higher in bookstores than in similar volume stores selling other products. More than most other categories of merchandise sold, books move in small quantities into and out of the stores. The economics of the book trade often make it a precarious profession. Bookstore owners and managers have to work hard.

Still, there is something about working with books and selling books that makes more and more people want to be booksellers. Under the right conditions and management, book-selling can be very rewarding. A love of books and knowledge of their contents is helpful in the trade, but in the end a bookstore is only as good as its management.

In my experience, the roof rarely caves in to create an extraordinary emergency, but it is the many little things that go wrong that accumulate when not taken care of and build into a big problem. Correctly or poorly handled, the little details have a great effect on bottom-line profit.

Booksellers should not just sit and wait for something to happen. Planning ahead is needed to help avoid the problems. The setting of policies, procedures, objectives, and financial goals will help prepare everyone on the staff to take the right actions and make proper decisions when expected and unexpected events occur.

That is what this book is about. It is not a textbook on bookselling; rather, it is a collection of ideas and principles that might be used to help booksellers manage better. The book contains basic policies and procedures, along with many of my personal axioms. I have tried to present interesting incidents and transactions that take place often in stores, accompanied by suggestions as to how to look at and handle them. Many are answers to questions raised at ABA Booksellers Schools and other meetings and seminars. Some have come out of my personal consulting work. I believe all of them to be practical ideas and tips for successful bookselling. Not all booksellers will agree with everything I suggest, but I hope this book will make some merchants think about the operation of a bookstore in a different way, and perhaps help make it more successful.

1

Becoming a Bookseller

Hardly a month goes by that I am not called for advice and information about getting into the bookstore business. Some of these prospective merchants have the necessary funds and an adequate knowledge of retailing to support their chances of success. Many are novices, however, with mistaken assumptions about bookselling. Some will make it, usually with a struggle; many others will fail within five years because of inexperience and lack of sufficient capital to grow the business. Reading, preparation, and goal-setting should be the first steps, with ideas and procedures for success spelled out in a business plan. (I might add that a trip to ABA Booksellers School is also advisable.) Your business plan should focus on location, a realistic budget, and expert management, the major ingredients for a profitable bookstore.

SETTING UP SHOP

Choosing a Location

One crucial factor that will help determine the success of a bookstore is location. Informed booksellers situate themselves where the book buyers are. People seeking a location for a new bookshop may shy away from shopping districts that already have one or more bookstores, believing that they will have a better chance to succeed without competition. But while it is true that some small markets can support only one bookshop, each area should be analyzed fully before being rejected. Ironically, the more bookstores established in a region, the greater the chance that another store will fit in too, particularly one with the right specialization. A good, well-used library nearby is another sign of a sound book market.

When selecting a site, keep in mind your potential customers—who they might be, where they come from, where they shop, and why they would shop in your store. Convenience is generally high on the list of priorities. In most areas, the ideal store would provide plenty of nearby parking at no charge and a safe area for patrons to walk and drive in, with good night lighting. It helps if the store is easy to find and close to surrounding residential areas. A one-stop shopping area with all kinds of stores is an ideal place to open a store. Consider malls, although the rent is often high. And beware of shopping centers with many vacancies; this usually means that the businesses located there do not do well.

Never underestimate the importance of visibility when choosing a site. A new retail store should be seen by as many people as possible to attract walk-in traffic, which will in turn create impulse purchases, a major part of sales. Initially, a high advertising budget may also be necessary to alert customers to the store's location, and even then, building a clientele can be a slow process.

Signing a Lease

Once a site has been chosen, the novice bookseller is advised to seek the help of knowledgeable people, both in bookselling and real estate law, before signing the lease. Some booksellers have lost their investment money quickly because of incorrect estimates of first-year sales, expenses, and type of market, all of which tie in to the potential lease terms. As a rule of thumb, rent should not exceed 10 percent of sales. Be on the lookout for potential additional costs, such as occupancy charges for common area maintenance and mandatory merchants' association fees, and make sure to factor in annual basic rent increases in line with the Consumer Price Index. Such charges could add 3 to 6 percent of sales in space costs. Remember that once a lease is signed, rent is a fixed cost.

Buying a Store

When acquiring an existing bookstore, know what you are buying. Most such transactions pertain to the buying and selling of solid, measurable assets—mainly fixtures, equipment, and, most important, inventory. In some cases, a goodwill payment is involved.

The seller's inventory should be inspected carefully by an experienced person before a price is determined. Often, the buyer finds that he or she has overpaid for the stock on hand; this leaves the bookseller in the unenviable and costly position of disposing of the bad stock and ordering new inventory. On average, 8 to 10 percent of any bookstore's inventory is unsalable at times during the year. The stock of a store about to be sold will often be considerably more out of date, with about 20 to 50 percent of inventory made up of deadwood or slow-moving books. From my experience, the following holds true:

(1) The average worth of the inventory being purchased is 30 to 40 percent of retail.

(2) After close inspection, a less-than-average inventory is worth 10 to 25 percent of retail. A better-than-average stock could be worth 40 to 50 percent of retail.

(3) Never pay full-cost price for a bookstore inventory. (A total stock brought into a store just one month ago costing 60 percent of retail is not worth more than 50 to 55 percent of retail today. I would pay as much as 55 percent of retail for someone else's brand-new stock only because the transportation is already paid.)

STOCKING THE SHELVES

Once a location has been chosen and the lease or contracts signed, study the demographics of the book market to learn about the kinds of books that should dominate the inventory. The book market for a particular location could have a radius of 1, 6, or even 30 miles. Much depends on the density of the local population and the nearness of other bookstores. A specialized bookshop can draw customers from more distant areas if it has the widest and deepest selection of its primary categories in the region. The following demographic elements will help a bookseller decide what kind of books to stock: population, income levels, education levels, principal occupations, age groupings/families, sex and marital status, home prices and rental costs, ethnic categories, and the kind of area (business, university, industrial, financial, residential). An in-depth discussion of stocking the store can be found in chapter 2.

MANAGING YOUR INVESTMENT

It is not enough to equip a store with merchandise, fixtures, and books and then open the doors to the public—prosperity does not necessarily follow. The most important element of the successful store is good management. A skillful manager plans, anticipates, organizes, and uses past history to create an efficient and profitable operation. Deficient management can lead to poor stock replacement, inferior customer service, inadequate employee direction, and mediocre displays—in other words, meager sales.

First-rate bookstore managers are competent supervisors, know when to delegate tasks, are detail-oriented, motivate their staff to perform efficiently, and have a commitment to profit and growth of the business. Managers who get the most done are those who organize their time well. Two important factors in managing time well are priority and delegation. The manager should know exactly what needs to be done at all times and how long each task may take. Successful managers accomplish tasks, or get others to accomplish them, on or ahead of schedule. And the more detail work that is delegated, the more time the manager will have to do the main job of controlling and growing the business.

2

Stocking the Store

A nyone can buy books to fill a bookstore. With the tremendous number of titles available, however—and almost forty thousand new selections each year—choosing the right books to stock is problematic. Buying wisely, based on the books' selling history, is the key to success for many bookshops. Effective buyers have a good grasp of the factors that lead to having the right books, in the right quantities, at the right times. These factors include knowing which titles will sell and when to stock them, purchasing quantities related to planned sales, and recognizing what is not selling and disposing of excess titles and quantities. This should result in the efficient movement of books into and out of the bookstore. In this chapter you will find many helpful tips for better buying.

DECISIONS IN BOOK BUYING

There are two major areas of book buying. One comprises books that were previously in stock and sold well. Their sales history can be used to decide the reorder quantity.

The other aspect of book buying involves new publications and titles with no prior sales history. Whether to stock and how many to stock demand analysis of the subject, author, and other details, as well as examining the sales record of similar books. The price, jacket, publisher's promotion, and format will all influence the number of copies to be ordered. In some cases, a new book has no useful characteristics to help make the decision. The buyer will inevitably miss some titles that should have been ordered and select some that produce no sales. The important point to remember is that stocking the store should never become automatic; time must always be taken to analyze new publications.

For years I have been urging booksellers to pay more attention to the basic titles in their inventory. One of the most fundamental principles of retailing is to replace basic stock. Although 75 percent of annual bookstore sales are derived from 25 percent of the titles, it is not advisable to reduce the stock of these slower-moving, but selling, titles. These are the books that attract a good deal of traffic to the store and build a reputation for "availability." Stocking one or two copies each of hundreds of titles that sell two to four copies a year pulls in the real book buyers, who purchase 5, 10, and 25 or more books a year. They are the browsers who make impulse purchases. Most of the great independent bookshops in the country grew because the owners and store buyers understood the importance of great selection.

Responding to What's Happening on the Sales Floor

A good book buyer is not wed to a desk but is close to the customers—on the sales floor listening to their requests, helping staff identify and satisfy customer wants, and getting a feel for market trends. The person who does the reordering knows the most about the stock and can provide invaluable information about the titles moving into and out of the store, thereby saving and creating sales.

All staff members, and of course the buyer, should be curious about repeat requests for books not stocked. Books are always being recommended by local doctors, psychologists, church people, teachers in schools and adult education classes, leaders in private clubs, and the like. Many of the basic stock titles in bookstores today became popular in this way. For every request or special order, there are other people who would buy these titles if they were displayed in stock.

When buying books in a series, each title should be considered on its own merits for stocking purposes, just like any other individual title. Four or five titles in each series are always in greater demand than others. Replace what sells. Do not stock all titles in the series in equal quantities, and don't make the mistake of assuming that it makes no difference which title in the series you keep in stock because if you don't have one, the customer will buy another. Customers usually come in with a specific title in the series in mind and will not be satisfied with a substitute.

In addition, be sure the "open-to-buy" is never closed. I really believe that most department stores lost the book business to other bookstores in the 1960s and 1970s because their managements were too strict with the book buyers. Their directive was that no more purchases could be made until overstocks were corrected. My axiom is that you should never be closed to buying what is needed now. Of course, you should work to rid the inventory of dead stock; but if you are out of copies of too many of the titles that customers are asking for, your business will go elsewhere.

Tips from Publishers and Sales Reps

Get along with the publishers and their sales representatives. Cooperating with publishers in the distribution of books will often result in "extras." The reps might know about warehouse overstocks or cooperative advertising available for a local book. Question your reps—find out what titles from their list sell well and what your competitors are selling that you are not. Reps may be able to advise you of regional titles or special promotional materials. Buyers who cooperate with their reps gain in the end.

Rules for Buying

Many years ago I created a word—SMOWS—to emphasize that booksellers should "sell more of what's selling." Too many book merchants are more concerned with potential returns than with knowing and acting on the current movement of stock. Stock control procedures should be established to alert the buyer to any special movement of titles or to changes in the speed of sales of titles. Fifty titles sold today have a better chance of selling tomorrow than all other titles on hand. And stocking more of what's selling produces more profit by creating more impulse sales.

Successful buyers *do* go out on a limb once in a while with a larger than expected order for a new novel or a nonfiction book by a new author. Usually some feature of the book strikes a chord. This intuition can be, and often is, correct, but buyers should always keep in mind expected sales when ordering books. Never stock a title because of an extra discount, free copies, free shipping, a pleasant sales rep, or attractive return privileges.

A buyer's personal likes and dislikes should not overrule the tastes of his or her customers. At the same time, the management should be aware of stock that is not suitable for its main market. For example, in a family-type bookshop in a family-oriented shopping center it is not necessary to stock and display a large selection of so-called "adult books," even though individual customers may want those titles. The books can be special ordered if requested.

Tools for Buying

It is important to know what buying tools are available and to use them to best advantage. Tremendous help can be found in the spring and fall announcement issues of both *Publishers Weekly* and *American Bookseller*. I also look through the supplier ads in these magazines. In addition, your file of filled and unfilled orders to publishers in the last six months can be valuable. Looking at previous orders can remind you of titles needed. A quick glance at any of these tools can help identify those few books that turn a small order earning a short discount into an order with a full trade discount.

It took me too long to realize that all well-reviewed books do not produce more sales. Occasionally a new publication becomes a good seller that way, but the buyer should beware of reviews in literary publications by authors and academicians addressing other writers and scholars in their respective professions. Often, only a small part of the potential market is reached in this way. On the other hand, titles mentioned in less-specialized general and news publications can draw customer interest and create sales. Reviews by popular or famous figures acclaiming a new title in any field often garner great interest in a title from a large segment of the book market.

Some booksellers are unhappy when new and local authors bring in their manuscripts and self-published books. These should not necessarily be ignored. No doubt handling most of them is a waste of time, but in my experience, 5 to 10 percent pay off. Why not inspect these walk-in books and, using your buying experience, choose some for display "on consignment"? Ask the authors if they have lists of friends who might be interested in their works and promote the book in a small mailing to those friends. Consider a party for a personable author. Some booksellers make a conscious effort to find local authors and their works through clubs, rotary groups, churches, and the local library.

Stocking University Press Titles and College Coursebooks

Many bookstore buyers do not pay enough attention to university press titles. It is true that most press books are addressed to the scholarly market and offer very short trade discounts that deter booksellers from even trying them. There are titles on many press lists that *do* fit the general bookstore market, however, and some of them have full trade discounts. Even a short-discount press book that relates to the main categories of the store or the region should be considered. I'm sure that many of the university titles would be well represented in bookstores if they were available from established trade publishers.

Should a trade bookstore stock college coursebooks? I usually reply to this question with a categorical "no." General bookshops will find it difficult to compete with the official campus or other complete college stores in selling required and recommended course titles.

Three branch managers, acting as buyers, once called me in early September and said they had ordered some coursebooks at the request of local instructors, who had come into their stores crying that the campus store never had enough copies of books for their classes or failed to get them in on time. The teachers promised to send all their students to those bookstores. But the store managers had no experience with student habits and, sure enough, the students went to the campus or other college stores first. The branch stores were left with most of their copies.

If you want to be involved with curriculum titles, cherry-pick them according to your regular market, concentrating on familiar trade titles, especially paperbacks. Add a few more copies of each to your stock at school opening times, including dictionaries and other reference books. Watch out for short discounts. And remember the high cost of transportation and handling of unsold books, returnable or not.

Getting Titles Fast

Use the telephone, fax, PUBNET, or other electronic services to order needed books. Some buyers do not like to order books by phone or fax, especially if they cannot use a toll-free number, but the changing speed-of-sale of books demands quick action. A call or fax can save three days to three weeks in obtaining needed stock. The first extra copy sold will pay for the call in most cases and the profit on additional sales is a bonus. In addition, more and more book merchants are using local and other speedy wholesalers to obtain needed books. A sale at a lesser trade discount is more profitable than no sale. Remember to use ESP—"emergency stock pronto."

There has also been a dramatic increase in the number of vendors offering electronic ordering. In addition to PUBNET, which facilitates direct electronic orders to most major trade publishers, an increasing number of wholesalers are now offering the option of electronic ordering to their customers. While such systems are not without problems, most companies indicate that retailers can place electronic orders 24 hours a day and receive confirmation in the same call. This can go a long way toward ensuring that you have a steady source of supply to satisfy customer needs.

SIDELINES

Products other than books, known as sidelines, may be stocked and sold profitably in a bookstore. There are valid arguments for and against sidelines in the bookstore, but I personally do not favor the sale of other major lines. I think they reduce the image of a dominant book selection and too much sideline display can make many customers wonder what the main business is. This is especially true of the small- to average-sized stores. Sidelines also require a disproportionately large display area and are usually nonreturnable.

On the other hand, sidelines may be a good customer draw, and can even be viewed as an added service. Another advantage is that sidelines generally have higher mark-ups and can be extremely profitable.

If you do decide that there is a demand and that you have the space for sidelines, there are many items to be considered. Some booksellers concentrate on one category, while others stock a selection of sidelines. The following four groups, in my experience, are both lucrative and comparatively easy to merchandise:

(1) *Calendars*—almost all bookstores now feature a variety of calendars in the last few months of the year.

(2) *Magazines*—with the upward spiral of cover prices, many booksellers are realizing the benefits of turnover, in a small space, even though the discounts are low. Keep in mind the retail display allowance available to merchants who display popular periodicals in an attentive way. Some booksellers do not believe it is worth the inconvenience of keeping records of sales, but no matter how small, the total rebate of about ten percent is all net profit.

(3) *Book Accessories*—bookmarks, bookplates, book covers, bags, and holders are convenient to display and have good markups.

(4) *Greeting Cards*—I suggest a few lines of special and unusual cards. If space is a problem, a complete selection may take up too much room.

Other sidelines to be considered, if there is an unfilled market and excess space, are maps and globes; games and toys; records, tapes, and video items; and prints and posters. Another potentially profitable sideline is packing and wrapping material; most of the items in this category offer very high markups. Jiffy and other mailing envelopes, gift boxes, papers and ribbons, wrapping paper, tapes, and other packing materials also seem to be in growing demand.

INVENTORY MANAGEMENT

Reordering

The policy of collecting reorders and waiting for a visit from the suppliers' reps has always bothered me. Often this is done to gain an extra discount; however, sometimes the reps are not expected for weeks, leading to far too many out-of-stock situations. Sales are lost both on books requested by customers and on impulse sales made when browsers notice books on the shelves.

The stealthiest thief in a store could be the wanted title that is out of stock. Day after day that gaping, unfilled display hole costs money in rent and other expenses, while robbing the bookshop of sales and profit. Some system of stock control should be used routinely to help keep those moving titles in inventory. Whether it is a manual or machine procedure, concentrating on the bread-and-butter items will help avoid the cardinal sin in retailing—being out of stock too often.

How do I know how many to reorder? This is a question asked constantly by buyers. Electronic control systems demand a specific answer to program the computer properly. Whatever control system is used, the same four quantity components should be examined to determine the reorder quantity:

(1) *Sales*—Recent sales are the primary factor to be studied. How many were sold in the past month and week, and, most important, in the past few days?

(2) *Basic On-Hand*—This is the minimum amount you want on hand at any given time to fill all requests for the title. The quantity sold over the past few months will help decide this figure.

(3) *Supplier Time*—How long does it take for the supplier to process the reorder? How many copies might sell in that time?

(4) *Delivery Time*—How many copies might sell between the time the order leaves the supplier's dock and the time it's placed on sale?

These four components total "stock to be provided," which can be used by the buyer for each title in the following reorder formula:

Reorder = Stock to Be Provided *minus* Stock on Hand
minus Outstanding Stock Orders

Another frequently asked question is "how long should I buy for?" The answer will depend on how much and how well the buyer has learned about the movement of orders from various suppliers. Other factors are the turnover goal and capital available. For periodic reorders of basic titles, ordering a three to four month supply is average, although many booksellers shave this to two to three months, especially if a large segment of their stock is obtained from nearby sources. New titles demand a lot of guesswork, but for titles expected to be bestsellers or to sell very well, it is more important to buy a larger quantity for a shorter period of time.

One of the main reasons buyers overstock new titles is the bestseller syndrome. Booksellers talk and think about the big books and lose sight of the duds and disappointments. Afraid of missing the next big book, they forget that the smash hit is the exception rather than the rule. Even if you are sure a book will be a bestseller, don't buy all the copies you expect to sell in a year on the first order. Remember that the average number of copies sold during the year of all titles stocked is probably between two and four.

Buyers tend to think not only about the bestsellers, but also about the top categories and the best sales months. That's fine as long as the stock of titles, categories, and total inventories reach their highest amounts in the weeks just before the peak sales. But the low points must be remembered too, and the stock on hand must be reduced at points when sales are expected to decline. That is why the most recent speed-of-sale is so important when reorders are being assessed. Thinking ahead and making a merchandise plan, including end-of-month inventories that relate to future months' sales, will be helpful. If you expect lower volume in July and August, buy more conservatively in the two or three months ahead, and then increase purchases August through October for the peak sales of November and December.

Overstocking

In my work with hundreds of booksellers over the years, I have found that nine times out of ten, problems stemmed from having too much stock rather than too little. I rarely recommend reducing the number of titles; selection should be retained. But cutting the number of copies will reduce overstock with the least detrimental effect on sales. Why get in the habit of ordering in lots of 3 when 2 might be sufficient, for example, or 25 when 18 would be enough? It is surprising how fast overstocks will be reduced, while concurrently increasing cash flow and display space and reducing handling time and transportation costs for getting and returning unsold books.

Overstocking is a major cause of retail store failure, especially bookstores. There are many expenses related to unsold and slow-moving books, increasing both the cost of goods sold and operating expenses, and resulting in reduced operating profit. Factors affecting operating profits include the following:

Cost of Sales—Incoming and return transportation and markdowns of dead books reduce gross profit. Penalties on some returns reduce credits, also reducing profit.

Operating Expenses—Employee time spent receiving, checking, pricing, recording, displaying, and processing returns of overstocks adds to wage expense and reduces profit.

Unmeasurable Effects—Bad or inappropriate books in inventory sometimes hide good books, losing potential sales. If specific books are brought in for special occasions, annual events, holiday and seasonal themes, and the like, consider reducing the prices to sell off overstocks rather than storing the books for a year.

Overstock is expensive to keep. It is like unspendable money sitting on the shelves and must be eliminated. The faster we recognize slow movers and dead stock, the more money we will realize from them. The longer we hold on to them to avoid admitting our buying mistakes, the higher will be the markdowns and the greater the chance that the returns privilege offered by the publishers will be lost.

One advantage that bookselling has over other kinds of retailing is that overstocks can be reduced relatively quickly. Getting rid of unsalable books by marking them down is efficient because it saves communication time with suppliers, bookkeeping work, and handling costs. But lots of dead stock cannot be sold at even close to half price; it is then more advantageous to return these copies for credits or refunds to be used for buying other books.

When end-of-month inventories are too high for several months, the following ways to reduce stock should be considered:

(1) more conservative buying of new titles and reorders;

(2) more liberal returns to suppliers (this could include an additional 100 percent inspection of inventory to eliminate dead stock and some slow-moving quantities);

(3) more extensive clearance from stock of nonreturnable books for a markdown sale; and

(4) having a special sale offering 10 or 20 percent off either all purchases or featuring a particular department.

For many years I advised booksellers to return most of their overstock books to suppliers rather than marking them down. My reasoning was that there is no item of merchandise deader than a dead book; therefore, you could generally recoup more from credits than from markdown sales. My thinking has changed because of the increasing costs of transportation and labor. To take advantage of both markdowns and returns:

(1) Mark down overstocks to 25 to 50 percent off, according to each title's value, and promote them on a clearance table for two or three weeks.

(2) Then reduce the marked-down titles that remain to 50 to 60 percent off retail and promote them for a week or two.

(3) All books unsold after three or four weeks should be returned for credit or refund to suppliers if in good condition.

My suggested annual goal, to keep inventory handling profitable for the average trade bookstore, is:

Returns to Resources . . . . .8.0% to 15% of purchases
Markdowns for Clearance . . . . . . .0.5% to 1.0% of purchases
Total Overstock . . . . .8.5% to 16% of purchases

Different kinds of bookshops will vary the ratio of returns and markdowns. Some stores tend to mark down most over-stocks because they have a market that will accept those books at about 50% or more of the original prices. Some shops that major in paperbacks might return most of the unsalable books. If overstocks amount to 18% or more, buying habits and proce-dures should be examined and more conservative purchasing considered. If unsold stocks total less than 8%, lost sales should be noted of titles and categories for future additions to inven-tory. And remember—disposal of non-sellers opens up buying dollars for more good books, and unsalable books ofteñ hide books that customers want.

Keep a keen eye on the back room. The receiving–shipping–stock area is one of the key operating points of a bookstore. Sales are lost if incoming merchandise is not processed on schedule. Special orders, new titles, special deliveries, and the like should be rushed to the sales area. Returns to publishers should not waste away in the corner, and extra stock should be monitored almost daily. No invoice or packing slip enclosed; mistakes in titles, quantities, and prices; too busy to attack a large receiving; one of four box truck freight missing—these are no excuse for not getting books onto the sales floor. Procedures should be set up to clear the receiving area of all needed titles by each evening; it can be done over 90 percent of the time.

Movement of Merchandise

Careful control of the movement of merchandise into and out of the store is a main contributor to the success of the business. Losing control by not holding to a reasonable stock plan is a chief cause of unprofitability, and may even lead to a business' failure. Every manager should have a grasp of the total dollar investment in the current inventory and what it might be in the near future. Using an automated system or a manual recording procedure, inventory should be budgeted based on the formula:

Beginning Inventory + Purchases − Sales = Ending Inventory

At the end of each month, the buyer should have a ballpark figure of stock on hand to adjust near-future purchases that will keep the inventory as close to the budget plan as possible. The following example is a six-month merchandise plan of the first half-year for a $200,000 annual volume bookstore.

	A Purchases	B Sales	C EOM Inventory
Beginning Inventory	—	—	70,000 (Jan. 1)
January	5,000	15,000	60,000
February	10,700	11,700	59,000
March	12,600	12,600	59,000
April	15,300	13,800	60,500
May	14,100	14,600	60,000
June	13,300	17,000	56,300
Totals	71,000	84,700	424,800*

* The average inventory is 424,800 divided by 7, or 60,685.

$$\text{Turnover} = \frac{\text{Sales}}{\text{Average Inventory}} = \frac{84,700}{60,685} = 1.40 \text{ (for one-half year)}$$

NOTES:

1. Purchases are actually listed in months of expected arrival; time estimates made by the buyer.

2. EOM (End of Month) inventories are budgeted after sales are projected, and made to approximate an average inventory desired by management when related to sales.

3. After B (sales) and C (EOM inventories) are budgeted, it becomes simple arithmetic to budget purchases, month by month. For example: EOM inventory for March is 59,000, minus April sales of 13,800, equals 45,200. But we planned to end April with 60,500; therefore, we must bring in 15,300 stock in April.

4. The 1.40 turnover in six months is reasonable. The second half-year usually attains higher volume and turnover, which could result in a turnover of about three for the year.

5. As the months pass, results should be compared to the plan so that future purchases can be adjusted to keep the budget on course. If sales and/or purchases differ from the plan, EOM inventory will be higher or lower than budget, and near-future purchases should be adjusted accordingly. For example: If April 1 (March 31) inventory is 58,000, it is 1,000 lower than plan. If April purchases (stock arrivals) are 15,000, they are 300 lower than plan. If sales in April are 14,000, they are 200 more than plan. Therefore EOM April inventory would be 59,000, 1,500 less than plan. That extra 1,500 could be ordered in May. It is a good idea to write each month's actual results next to the plan figures on the chart. Merchandise ordered in one month might arrive over three months' time in many cases.

6. *IMPORTANT*—the trend of sales should be watched for major changes in the market. Continued higher or lower sales than planned should alert the buyer to change the purchase budget for many months ahead, so as not to become understocked or overstocked, since these are factors that could affect future business.

Turnover

I have always preached the importance of "availability"—having the best selection in the market. I would also rather be 5 to 10 percent overstocked occasionally than 5 to 10 percent understocked. Therefore, I prefer a turnover rate in the lower range rather than the higher. What is a good turnover number? I suggest two-and-one-half to three-and-one-half turns a year for the average general bookstore. In that range, you can provide a very good selection with a reasonable investment and can display and handle the inventory well if sales are under $300 per square foot. Bookstores with good stock control procedures can attain higher turnovers profitably. The important points to think about are:

(1) An unexplained high turnover number could mean lost sales because of inadequate selection. If you suspect your turnover rate is too high, I would suggest analyzing the buying procedures and details to make sure the store is not out of too many titles.

(2) A very low turnover could mean costly returns, over-stocking with bad books hiding good books, wasted investment, and excessive markdowns. If turnover is near two or below, I would question the buyer's usage of the bookstore's stock control plan, or establish a system if none exists.

There has been much discussion in recent years suggesting that higher turnover means greater profit. That is not always true. The main advantages of better turnover are less dollars tied up in inventory, less space needed, and higher return on investment. The reduced interest cost on the investment creates more profit. However, many of the largest and most successful independent booksellers have grown their businesses with a turnover between two and three by having the greatest selection of titles in the region—attracting more and more customers with the reputation "they have the book if any store has it." Of course, these stores had efficient buying procedures that kept markdowns and returns within acceptable ranges, while the extra interest cost on the slower-moving inventory reduced profit percent on sales. The important point is that these booksellers accepted less percentage profit to build the volume, at the same time attaining more profit dollars.

My advice—especially to new bookselling entrepreneurs—is do not get hung up on high turnover while building the business. Attain the most out of the potential market. You do not automatically increase profit by increasing turnover while volume stands still.

Take, for example, two bookstores that open for business at the same time. Store A is conservative and builds volume slowly over the next two years, keeping inventory at a constant level with the aim of higher turnover, which increased from 3.0 to 3.4 in the third year. Operating profit percentage remains the same as profit dollars increase slightly. This is the profit and loss result:

	STORE A					
	1st Year		2nd Year		3rd Year	
	$	%	$	%	$	%
Sales	300,000		320,000		340,000	
Cost of Sales	180,000	(60)	192,000	(60)	204,000	(60)
Gross Profit	120,000	(40)	128,000	(40)	136,000	(40)
Operating Expenses	100,000	(33.3)	106,500	(33.3)	113,300	(33.3)
Operating Profit	20,000	(6.7)	21,500	(6.7)	22,700	(6.7)

Store B is more aggressive after attaining the same first-year results as Store A. The owner adds $25,000 retail inventory ($15,000 cost) in both the second and third years, and wins the following results:

	STORE B					
	1st Year		2nd Year		3rd Year	
	$	%	$	%	$	%
Sales	300,000		350,000		400,000	
Cost of Sales	180,000	(60)	210,000	(60)	240,000	(60)
Gross Profit	120,000	(40)	140,000	(40)	160,000	(40)
Operating Expenses	100,000	(33.3)	116,550	(33.3)	133,300	(33.3)
Operating Profit	20,000	(6.7)	23,450	(6.7)	26,700	(6.7)
Less Interest on Extra Stock	—	—	1,000	(0.3)	2,000	(0.5)
Net Profit	20,000	(6.7)	22,450	(6.4)	24,700	(6.2)

NOTES:

1. Store B turnover fell from 3 to 2.7 in the third year.
2. However, Store B had sales $60,000 higher than Store A.
3. Store B's profit dollars were higher than Store A's in both the second and third years.
4. Even though Store B's net profit percent fell from 6.7 to 6.2 by the third year, many booksellers would prefer Store B's results.

The owner and/or manager must watch all factors to balance turnover with extra investment and profit results. In addition, as sales rise, operating expenses should decline as a percentage of sales, leaving even more profit dollars that can be used to pay off loans faster, reducing interest costs. Gross profit should also increase because of larger stock orders. (These percentages have been shown as constant in the above examples.)

AVOIDING BUYING PITFALLS

Some miscellaneous tips for book buyers:

(1) Know who you are dealing with. Be aware of orders that have not been filled by suppliers. Most problems are with small, new, or unknown distributors that advertise titles not available, collect orders until enough are received to reprint a title, and fail to answer inquiries. Many grievances relate to books received in an unexpected format, credits not received for returned books, excessive increases in prices from those listed, and prepayments made that are not refunded when the order was not filled. Do not make payments to unfamiliar suppliers until service has been received.

(2) When returning damaged or defective books, clearly mark the chargeback "DO NOT REPLACE." It might take months to receive a replacement shipment, if received at all. If you do want to replace the copies, include them on your next order, with no reference to the returned copies. That is the best way to keep the record straight on both ends.

(3) Do not finalize an order with a supplier for trade books that would earn less than a 40-percent discount without searching for salable titles to add to the order for a full discount. Check basic title lists, previous orders, and the complete catalog if necessary. Even special orders can be added to stock orders to earn better terms for both. Combining orders has a great impact on cost of sales, increasing gross profit. In addition, for every package of small shipments eliminated, postal dollars are saved. But note, as discussed earlier, if no appropriate titles can be found, do not delay a much-needed order. Sales at a lower discount are better than no sales at all.

SUMMARY

Allow me to conclude this section on buying by emphasizing once again that bookselling is a title business. If a book is not in stock at your store, most customers will look for it elsewhere. A large selection of titles is more important than having many copies of each title.

Another key to success is having stock control procedures in place to record the movement of books. Systems can be simple and inexpensive, or complex and costly—whatever procedures are used, however, the manager must feel comfortable with them and trust them to keep out-of-stock items to a minimum. The stock control procedures should provide the buyer with daily, weekly, and monthly information. The recent movement history and speed-of-sale of books are important factors that influence the buyer's decisions. And remember—a good head for buying and a sharp eye for inventory management can mean a successful, prosperous bookstore.

3

Customer Service

Although owners and managers enter their bookstores countless times each year, it is very difficult to step back and see the shop through the eyes of the customers. A bookstore should be welcoming in both appearance and atmosphere. More people stop shopping at a store because of employee indifference than for any other reason, and a bookstore manager cannot take good customer relations for granted. Periodically, an owner and/or manager should take the time to assess service policies and procedures, with an eye toward ensuring that customers have reason to be satisfied with the environment and service being offered.

EMPLOYEE–CUSTOMER RELATIONS

Be Kind to the Customer

For decades, customers have accepted self-service and self-selection in retail stores, albeit somewhat grudgingly; but now they are looking for, even demanding, better service and more courteous attention. At a time when many bookstores stock similar or the same books and sell them at about equal prices, shopper service becomes an important factor in attracting book buyers. An important component of customer service is expressed in the timeworn axiom, "the customer is always right"—one of the easiest policies the store can adopt, but often readily forgotten amidst hectic everyday business. It is surprising how little extra attention it takes to be courteous; even a small amount of enthusiasm will go a long way toward making regular customers out of browsers.

Keep in mind that customers are not all alike and should be treated as individuals. Just as you can't tell a book by its cover, you cannot categorize customers by their looks or by the clothes they wear. Treat them all as if they are about to buy hundreds of dollars worth of books, and thank them as if they did every time they leave the store.

Most bookstores do not need full-time cashiers, bookkeepers, advertising specialists, display experts, or computer professionals and usually cannot afford specialized employees until they attain very high sales volumes. Almost every staff member should be able to handle 80 to 90 percent of the store's functions. Make sure there is always a manager on hand, however, or a staff member acting as manager. Nothing irritates a customer more than being told that an exchange, credit, or some other common transaction cannot be completed because the manager is not available.

One service that can play a large part in encouraging—or discouraging—business is the store's return and exchange policy. You would not return to a store that made you feel uncomfortable, even if you finally did get a credit. Set a reasonable policy for returns, credits, and cash refunds that will ensure happy customers. It's good business to exchange a salable book regardless of where it was purchased; after all, most books can be returned to the publisher.

Try to accommodate the customer's wishes. Break down a window display if those are the only copies of a requested title. This also applies to copies in a box just arrived in the receiving room—break it open! If the last copy of a wanted title in stock is damaged, mark down the price generously. The customer will usually accept the book gladly, at the same time enabling you to dispose of a hurt copy.

Booksellers should assure that each and every customer who leaves their bookstore feels totally satisfied with the purchases made. Every store policy and practice should be responsive to customers' desire for honest merchandising. You can fool some customers some of the time, but most of them are smarter than you might think.

Turning Service into Sales

Customers requesting assistance should always be accompanied by a staff member to the section where the books they want can be found. This enables the employee to suggest other appropriate books or secure a special order. If all staff members are busy helping customers and you have to ask the patron to wait, make sure he or she knows that you'll soon be available. Never let a customer leave your store angry because of lack of interest on the part of the staff.

Salespeople do not have to be literary critics. If a customer wants a title but the staff member thinks another on the same subject is better, the employee should not disparage the requested book. *Do* recommend an additional purchase of the preferred book. Above all, do not use the hard-sell pressure tactics that most customers resent.

Handling Customer Complaints

Most bookstores receive lots of mail from customers, ranging from book orders to nasty complaints. It makes for good bookstore-customer relations to have a policy of answering all correspondence within 48 hours (or a reasonable time frame). If a book is not in stock, let the customer know that it has been ordered and how long it will take to receive it. If a question is asked or a problem stated that you cannot quickly resolve, let the customer know that you are seeking the answer, with information to follow. If there is a complaint, acknowledge the store's fault with apologies, and explain how you will remedy the problem to the patron's satisfaction; in fact, in certain cases a telephone call may be more helpful and calming to the customer. Believe it or not, some grievances can even be used as opportunities to produce happy book buyers. A complaint resolved quickly may have the complainer praising your bookshop to friends.

STORE SERVICES

Booksellers should flaunt the special store services they offer— gift wrapping, special ordering, mailing books, out-of-print book searches, and the like. Many customers make a point of shopping where they get such services, thus creating extra sales.

Special Orders and Search Services

Special ordering is practically essential in bookselling to make available to patrons the thousands of books that cannot be stocked in the store. It is a great way to keep the customers coming back, and it gives the bookstore an edge over the discounters and chains, many of which do not offer such services. Working with special orders also helps build book knowledge and provides ideas for titles to be added to the store inventory. If the profits on special orders are not adequate for your business, service and postage fees can be charged. Keep in mind that many of the benefits of fulfilling special orders may not be immediately reflected in your profit–loss figures.

Another good sideline is an out-of-print book search service. An up-front service charge can pay for the expense; if a copy is found, a very profitable markup will also be earned.

Charge Accounts

Although each bookseller should evaluate the needs of his or her clientele, I would counsel against offering personal charge accounts. Store charge accounts require substantial bookkeeping and paperwork, with additional staff hours, and often produce collection problems and write-offs. Instead, I would recommend accepting two or three of the main bank or other credit cards and promoting them as a service. There is enough credit-card competition to keep fees reasonable, and it is a faster and simpler procedure than trying to do all the accounting within the bookstore.

Special Discounts

The decision to offer special discounts to schools, libraries, and businesses should be carefully thought out. Too often, small orders involve much work and time, especially if special orders are included, and do not warrant discounts of 20 percent or more off listed prices. Sometimes the order is so complicated that no discount should be given. Trying to win these orders away from wholesalers or other bookstores can result in more volume but little or no extra profit—the additional details involved might even distract a bookseller from the main job of operating and supervising the retail-store activities.

If these kinds of orders make up a large segment of your total business, however, bear in mind the following:

(1) once you give discounts, it is difficult to stop;

(2) size up the competition before deciding how much of a discount you will offer;

(3) determine the kind and dollar amount of orders that you will accept at discount;

(4) establish one discount policy for books in stock and a less liberal one for books to be special ordered; and

(5) once a policy has been established, it should be put in writing, made known to everyone on the staff, and followed.

EVALUATING STORE POLICIES

Often it is the little things we do that most please shoppers. Once booksellers weigh the benefits and disadvantages, they often find that easing certain restrictions makes shopping in their store a more pleasant experience. For example, perhaps you need not insist that all purchases be bagged before leaving the checkout counter, or you might allow customers to bring reasonable refreshments into the store. I would guess the potential markdowns would be far less than the profit on sales discouraged. Also, is it really essential to demand two or three kinds of identification before accepting checks on purchases? No doubt some restrictions are needed, but take the time to examine the regulations in your store and make sure their negative impact does not overshadow your store's positive image.

And why keep customers in the dark? One store action that is an irritant to me is the constant flickering of the store lights just before closing, while shoppers are still browsing—especially when it's done five or ten minutes before your advertised closing time. Don't discourage potential purchases.

The same applies to opening the store. If you find that at the start of the day you often have customers at the doors anxious to get in, consider opening the doors early. All too frequently, employees inside just ignore these prospective sales, some of which end up being lost. Putting in a little overtime, at both ends of the day, can get you satisfied customers.

SUMMARY

The bookstore that creates an image of courteous, friendly service has a great advantage over the competition that doesn't. Good customer service and selling practices are important elements in gaining loyal customers, who will, in turn, spread the word to fellow book buyers—and so it grows!

4

Financial Factors

M ost of my consulting work with booksellers involves financial matters. Over time, I have found that poor profits often result from unwarranted assumptions and inexperienced planning that take place even before the bookstore has opened. The majority of financial problems, however, are due to mismanagement of the dozens of money elements and fiscal decisions arising from the daily operations of a bookstore. Difficulties can emerge in the following five categories:

(1) budgeting;
(2) operating expense control;
(3) merchandise cost control or cost of sales;
(4) money handling and usage; and/or
(5) bookkeeping.

Intelligent analysis of well-kept records can aid a bookseller in making good financial decisions. There is also a new publication available from the American Booksellers Association— *ABACUS Expanded*—that provides financial profile data from almost 200 booksellers doing business in more than 250 locations. This book is useful in providing operational benchmarks for independent booksellers.

What follows are suggestions to improve financial results.

BUDGET

Effective budgeting is important to attain bookselling success. Budgeting involves planning and setting down on paper numbers that can be analyzed and compared to actual merchandising and operating results to see if the financial goals of management are on track. The larger the business, the more formal and detailed should be the budgeting process. Making, monitoring, and modifying a budget can help keep a bookstore on a profitable course, lessening the chances of failure.

A good budget maker will reason out all buying costs and operating expenses, focusing on the previous year's figures to establish new financial targets. A detailed, year-long profit and loss budget should be divided into months, with ballpark figures clearly marked for periodic monitoring against the budget. Variations from plan can be early warning signals, indicating that corrective action should be taken before financial problems grow to disastrous dimensions.

Designing a Budget: Case Example

There are five main components of a profit and loss statement. These are shown in the following sample budget for a bookstore with a previous year's annual sales volume of $300,000. The basic formula used to arrive at operating profit is:

Sales *minus* Cost of Goods Sold = Gross Profit *minus*
Operating Expenses = Operating Profit before Taxes

	Last Year's Results		This Year's Budget	
	$	%	$	%
Sales	300,000	100.0	324,000	100.0
Cost of Merchandise Sold	191,400	63.8	204,455	63.1
Gross Profit	108,600	36.2	119,555	36.9
Operating Expenses	104,700	34.9	111,590	34.4
Operating Profit	3,900	1.3	7,965	2.5

The new budget shows that management is planning to double its profits—but how can a bookseller estimate figures with any degree of accuracy? Simply stated, he or she scrutinizes last year's figures line by line, examining all factors that might be used to improve buying costs and operating expenses. All costs of operating a bookstore are measured against sales. Increased sales can compensate for some rising expenses, but we should not let that deter us from trying to be more efficient. Let's see how this manager arrived at the budget figures represented in the chart.

(1) Sales are planned to increase by 8 percent, a conservative number for a store that has been open for only two years. But it should be noted that a discount store opened six months ago that will be highly competitive. There will be some increase in sales from opening three nights each week instead of one, as the store now does. Last year's weather, special promotions, and economic conditions are among the factors that should be considered when budgeting sales.

(2) The cost of sales is made up of five elements:

Publishers' Discounts—the buyer believes that the cost of books can be decreased by 0.5 percent because he or she is now more experienced in taking advantage of publishers' terms. Specials and other small orders will be combined into larger orders for higher-quantity discounts.

Postage—the cost of freight into the store and on returns will be somewhat less when the buyer combines orders and eliminates many small packages. More efficient buying could reduce overstock returns.

Markdowns—these will be about the same as last year.

Shortage—also budgeted about the same as last year.

Cash Discounts—also budgeted the same as last year.

Therefore, the cost of sales is planned to decrease this year by 0.7 percent, from 63.8 to 63.1 percent. As a general rule, a reasonable range for cost of sales is 61 to 65 percent of sales.

(3) Gross profit will also improve by 0.7 percent to 36.9 percent. An acceptable range for gross margin is 35 to 39 percent of sales.

(4) Operating expenses is the area where management can either shine or let the business deteriorate. Here again, we budget by thinking how we can lower some expenses this year to help increase net profit. A store usually has a breakdown on the profit and loss statement of 10 to 20 different expenses. Total operating expenses should be 29 to 34 percent of sales. Here is how this bookseller analyzed the main expenses while planning for this year.

(a) Salaries and wages are usually the largest operating expense and the most controllable. It is the cost element attacked first by management when profit results are poor or trending down; for example, replacing one 40-hour full-time employee with two 15-hour part-timers. The owner or salaried manager may then have to fill in more hours on the selling floor.

(b) Rent is not controllable once the lease has been signed. If the total dollars remain the same, the percentage to sales will be lower on increased volume planned.

(c) Now that the bookstore is in its third year of operation, most people in the market know where it is and what kind of store it is. At this point the size and frequency of ads can be reduced somewhat, except for special promotions and sales to combat the discount image of the new, competitive store that opened recently. For example, the telephone book ad can be reduced in size. There will be better recordkeeping on advertising to obtain more co-op money from publishers.

(d) Electricity bills can be reduced a bit. When the staff is working on stock and displays before and after business hours, only half the lights will be on. Also, the window lights will be turned off at store closing, rather than at midnight.

(e) Telephone bills will be lower because the buyer will try to use toll-free numbers or call collect when placing orders.

(f) Supplies and stationery will be purchased at discount and variety stores at a 20- to 30-percent savings over commercial stationers.

(g) Other items like insurance, taxes, postage, and professional fees are budgeted the same or slightly higher.

Overall, reductions top increases, and total operating expenses will be reduced by 0.5 percent, from 34.9 to 34.4 percent.

(5) An acceptable parameter for operating profit is 4 to 8 percent before taxes. This result will usually provide a satisfactory return on investment to the owner, with funds to grow the business. In this particular case, however, the existence of stiff competition was noted, hence the conservative estimate for increase in sales and lower operating profit. Therefore, operating profit will increase from 1.3 to 2.5 percent on the budget for this year.

Putting the Budget to Work

The budget for this year is made and the basics of the plan conveyed to the employees. Now the figures should be monitored as monthly results are recorded. If there are significant variations from budget, some items on the next monthly budget should be considered for moderation. Minor variations might not demand change until a trend is noted over two or three months.

The most dangerous situation is when sales figures are behind plan. Management should analyze the reasons for the shortfall and consider moderating some expenses on the future months' budgets to bring the profit objective back into view. Buying may have to be reduced to keep markdowns and transportation costs on surplus books under control. An important point to remember is that any and all expense overages affect the operating profit. That is why results should be checked in detail periodically to offset the variations by moderating future plans. Other sections of this chapter will offer more tips on reducing expenses.

Effect of Inflation on Budget

Inflation—an increase in prices, sometimes sharp and sudden—should be considered when making profit and loss budgets, from top-line sales to bottom-line profits. There are many causes for inflation, including an extraordinary demand for certain items or a sudden lack of products that consumers want. Let's say, for example, that there is a great demand for retail space, which may force a bookseller to pay much higher rent to renew a lease. The electric company, maintenance and repair firms, stationery stores, and others from whom booksellers buy merchandise and services might have to raise their prices, thereby increasing the operating expenses of the bookseller.

The following chart shows the potential effects of inflation on a bookstore operation (all percentages based on sales). Last year's figures are for a $300,000 volume bookstore. This year's figures for the same store reflect inflation increases of 0.2 percent for transportation costs and 1.0 percent for operating expenses, with no sales increase. Next year's budget plan projects a 4.0 percent increase in sales and a 1.0 percent reduction in expenses to attain a better profit result.

	Last Year's Results		This Year's Budget		Next Year's Budget	
	$	%	$	%	$	%
Sales	300,000		300,000		312,000	
Cost of Sales	186,000	62.0	186,500	62.2	194,064	62.2
Gross Profit	114,000	38.0	113,500	37.8	117,936	37.8
Operating Expenses	102,000	34.0	105,000	35.0	106,080	34.0
Operating Profit	12,000	4.0	8,500	2.8	11,856	3.8

Notice how difficult it is to retain profit in an inflationary economy. Next year's budget, if met, will beat this year's results, but profit will still be less than last year's. It would take a larger sales increase than 4 percent and/or still lower operating expenses to equal or better last year's profits.

OPERATING EXPENSES

Payroll

When asked to help a bookshop that is having expense problems, the first component I usually look at is the payroll-to-sales ratio. Total wages, including a reasonable salary for a working owner, is the largest cost of doing business. Wages can easily account for 40 to 50 percent of total operating expenses. It is the first area to which professional retailers look for savings when profit is below plan. When economic conditions slow down sales growth, work hours are reduced to offset increasing noncontrollable expenses.

I once attended a retailing meeting at which a department store executive said that he often wished the high-cost employees, on the job for many years, who just perform adequately would resign. Then new hires could take their places at less cost and perform as well on average in most selling positions. Another manager commented that she would be glad to give up $30,000 or more in sales in a year and drop the cost of a full-time employee.

Sales of $30,000 minus $19,500 (cost of sales at 65 percent gross margin) equals $10,500. That leaves only $5 per hour for a full-time employee's pay plus benefits and other costs. That is why there is sometimes not enough help in stores, particularly on nights, weekends, and holidays; payroll is the motivating factor. Be aware, however, that a lack of good service and stock knowledge create shopper complaints, especially in department, chain, and other large stores.

Rent

What is the right rent? That is a question often asked by prospective booksellers. There are many factors that determine the acceptability of a rent cost, particularly the prospective sales volume and the sum of all the other expenses. Different kinds of bookstores can afford different ratios of rent to sales. The primary figure to consider is sales, which pays for all the costs of merchandise and the operating expenses.

My general answer to the question of reasonable rent is that rent (all space costs paid to landlord) should be less than 10 percent of sales, if all other expenses are budgeted to be average or higher. (It is a danger signal if most expenses are predicted to be above industry averages.) Average bookstore rent and related expenses are probably about 7 percent of sales volume. Below that figure, there is leeway to accept higher payroll or other expenses; higher rent means tighter control of other expenses.

There are many very successful bookshops in secondary and tertiary locations, with rent costs of only 2 to 5 percent of sales, that have built up great sales volume and customer loyalty because of their book selections. The desirability of the area may have changed but the customer draw is there, and the landlord does not want to risk losing a good tenant and perhaps not be able to re-rent the space. Sometimes the bookstore owner is the landlord. There are also bookstores with 12 percent or more rent costs, but other expenses, especially payroll, are low, allowing an acceptable profit. It is important to understand the relationship between sales and space when contracting for a location. Usually, the larger the space, the less cost per square foot. The newer the building and higher the demand for space in the area, the greater the cost. Here are some of my evaluations of affordable and problem rent costs:

Annual Sales	Total Space	Annual Rent	Rent to Sales	Sales per Square Foot	Comment
$100,000	1,200	$12,000	12.6%	$ 83.33	Dangerous
200,000	2,000	18,200	9.1	100.00	Just O.K.
300,000	2,000	30,000	10.0	150.00	Borderline
400,000	1,500	16,000	4.0	266.66	Excellent
600,000	2,000	40,000	6.7	300.00	Excellent
750,000	3,500	48,000	6.4	214.29	Good

The more efficiently a bookseller is using space, the higher will be sales per square foot, allowing for expanding volume at less rent cost. The more dense the inventory and space crowding, the more important it is to generate above-average turnover. A new bookshop should plan to achieve a minimum of $125 per square foot the first year, with room to reach $200 by the third or fourth year, and potential for at least $300 per square foot in the future. Inflation of prices will help, but remember that sales are the primary factor to be considered, from which all expenses should be estimated and related. An out-of-line sales figure can cause eventual bookstore failure.

Once a deal is made for the space cost, the large rent expense will be fixed, perhaps rising with sales but never decreasing. When operating profit is too low and expenses are reasonable except for a too-high rent-to-sales ratio, a trip to the landlord is in order. It will take all your selling, convincing, and negotiating skills, but it's worth trying rather than accepting a "killing" rent that is causing poor profit.

I was once called on to help out the owner of a small, established, independent bookshop in a community shopping center. The store's sales were increasing at less than cost-of-living rates, while annual profits were decreasing. After going over the financial statement, I found that the bookseller was achieving good cost-of-sales results; operating expenses, however, were at least 2 percent on sales higher than average for his kind and size of store and location. The money all seemed to go to rent, which had increased from 8 to 10 percent of sales over recent years. The lease terms were increasing the cost by $1,200 annually, $100 per month. A discussion with the book merchant revealed that there were always one or two store spaces vacant in the mall. I suggested that he go to the landlord, show him the profit and loss statements indicating the inadequate salary and profit picture, and explain that there would probably be another empty store if rent could not be moderated. After much discussion and deliberation, the landlord agreed to alter the lease terms to a straight 8 percent of annual sales.

Using Space Wisely

Although expensive, space is often wasted. It may be possible to gain more room in the store by changes in either merchandising display or fixturing. Overstocks could be returned to suppliers faster by inspecting the inventory more often. It would improve turnover and make space available to bring in potentially better sellers.

Utilize blank spaces on walls, posts, and ends of gondolas and tables as possible display areas. As for fixturing, most bookshops can create more shelf or table space by altering display stands in some way. Wall and gondola shelves may be set too far apart, leaving many inches bare above the tops of books. Five shelves on the wall might become six, and four on the gondola might become five, adding 20 percent or more space to those sections. Short gondolas can be raised by adding one or two shelves. Of course, all shelves should be adjustable to allow for more flexibility. Tables are useful, but if more space is needed, a one- or two-shelf addition can be added on top. If aisles are 54 to 72 or more inches wide, narrowing them might allow for an extra row of fixtures. If there are many short gondolas and/or tables with aisles around them, they could be pushed together end to end, creating more floor space for additional fixtures. Many stock-receiving rooms are much too large. If this area occupies more than 10 percent of total floor space, it might be compacted to create more selling area.

Keep in mind, however, when considering the above space-saving changes, that your store should be welcoming and comfortable for shoppers. If your changes would convey a negative feeling to customers, you might want to go back to the drawing board and re-evaluate how you can make the most of your space.

Everyday Expenses

When I fell into bookselling more than 50 years ago, I often wondered why the general manager was always so strict about how the staff used supplies, how they wrapped packages, how they weighed outgoing packages. He seemed to be looking over our shoulders constantly, even on menial tasks, to make sure we were not wasting anything. He often checked the water and lighting usage.

A few years later, when I was in charge and responsible for profit results, I came to understand the actions of my former boss. Some examples of small items that may add up to savings:

(1) Turn off at least half the lights when the store is closed and employees are working there.

(2) Save incoming boxes to use for returns to publishers.

(3) Know how to wrap gifts efficiently so as not to waste paper and ribbons.

(4) Check the postal scale periodically to make sure it is not overweighing (it never underweighs).

(5) Place occasional extra cash balances into interest-bearing money accounts. Combine bank accounts, if more than one, to save on bank fees and other charges. Remember, it is your money to spend and to save.

At one time or another, almost every bookseller has to purchase equipment, supplies, and services in large quantities or at high cost. The first price quoted should not be accepted immediately; instead, obtain bids. Don't always say to a company salesperson or an insurance agent, "just repeat last year's order," or "write out the same deal." The first time I obtained three premium costs on a package of insurance items the original agent found a way to quote a lower price to retain the contract.

I am surprised that so many booksellers waste money on supplies and other sundry items. There is no need to go to the full-price commercial stationers for daily staples like pencils, stationery, markers, and dozens of other articles available from discount and variety stores. The discount merchandise is usually of equal value at 25- to 40-percent savings. The low-margin home improvement stores can provide hammers, scissors, cleaning items, and small equipment at great savings. And why buy scratch pads when there is so much paper available in bookstores? Be a tightwad and let the saved dollars become bottom-line profit.

SALES

How much do sales grow in the first five years? I have been asked this question many times. My formula is that volume in the fifth year should be about double the first year's sales: a 30 percent increase the second year, 20 percent the third, 15 percent the fourth, and a 12 percent increase in the fifth year will result in double the sales of a new bookstore over five years (allowing for inflation). Some bookstores make it easily; others do not.

An Overview of Sales

We are all happy when sales go up, of course, and disappointed when they go down, but total sales are not the be-all and end-all to the financial success of a bookshop. Profitable volume pays for all the costs relating to the merchandise and of operating the business—but the sales volume sometimes hides management problems and high operating expenses. Very rapid sales growth might lead a bookseller to pay out too much for fixed expenses and capital investment—difficult expenses to reduce if sales level off. Annual volume increases of 10 to 20 percent might produce a safer future than a one-year jump of 40 or 50 percent in sales. In that way, the store's foundation will be built brick by brick, with less chance of collapsing under the weight of a heavy debt and uncontrollable expenses.

How do the months rate for sales and profit? A few years ago, I surveyed many general bookstores and a large chain; I believe the same figures apply today. The stores all had the same busy seasons, and no summer or winter resorts or other areas with special sales peaks were included. Although there were some large variations in the order of importance, the following reflects the average for all stores and shows how profit is related to sales volume:

	Sales			Profit	
1.	December	21.5%	1.	December	57.5%
2.	November	10.5	2.	November	10.0
3.	June	8.2	3.	June	7.5
4.	September	8.0	4.	September	5.0
5.	January	7.5	5.	October	3.0
6.	October	7.5	6.	March	3.0
7.	March	6.7	7.	January	2.5
8.	May	6.5	8.	February	2.5
9.	February	6.0	9.	April	2.5
10.	April	6.0	10.	May	2.5
11.	August	6.0	11.	July	2.0
12.	July	5.6	12.	August	2.0
		100.0%			100.0%

NOTE: November and December produce 30% to 35% of annual volume but 65% to 70% of annual profit.

The Extra Sale

Remember the power of suggestion. The profit realized from selling an additional title to a customer is greater than the profit on either the first sale or the average sale made in a bookstore. Why? Because almost all the gross profit on the second sale reaches the bottom-line operating profit. There is no additional staff expense and no extra utilities, insurance, taxes, or even rent charges, except for a slight charge if the lease requires it. Conversely, a lost sale for any reason—out of stock, misplaced, poor service—reduces the profit on the average sale. Therefore, a "saved" sale is also more profitable than the average sale over time.

Discounting

In recent years, booksellers have seen a decrease in sales due to discount competition. Some stores have counteracted the problem by stocking the largest collection of titles in their region. Others remain in good health through specialization and overwhelming the customers with book knowledge, service, and convenience. When those actions don't work, however, projecting the image of savings might be the only answer. Some bookstores have done this by expanding their bargain book departments containing remainders, reprints, and special buys. These kind of books make up 20 to 40 percent or more of the complete discounter, and they show your customer that you have the same bargains as the competition. Booksellers should determine the extent to which selling good sellers and active backlist books at a discount makes sense for their store. Such discounting should be controlled and monitored to ensure that the lost margin on the books is made up by the volume sold or the increased sales of full-price books.

Let's look at a specific example to see how discounting works. If you discount a $15.95 book that cost you $9.57, and sell it at $11.95, you give up $4.00 of the gross profit, leaving you $2.38. Here is what you might consider:

(1) Will you sell 2.7 times as many copies of that book to make up the full $6.38 gross profit, even though gross margin will be a little lower? Or will you make it up by selling an extra $10.00 book at full retail and one copy at discount to earn the

full $6.38? Either way you will be retaining customers and perhaps growing the business.

(2) If you do not discount and lose the sale and, perhaps, the customer, wouldn't it be better to sell the copy at discount even though some gross profit is lost?

(3) The more inventory that is discounted, the more important it is to keep operating expenses below conventional bookshop figures, while achieving higher turnover. Capital investment should also be lower. But to most independent booksellers already in business, building volume and dollar net profit are more important than attaining a high return on investment.

Fees for Special Services

Consider imposing special fees as a source of income that could be tapped to improve a poor profit picture. If a merchant has strong competition, it might not be workable to charge fees that do not prevail in the market. But it has come as a surprise to many booksellers that such charges have been accepted with little or no complaint over the past decade. Some bookstores charge $1.00 or more for a special order, for example, and 50¢ to $1.00 for special gift wrapping. Markup on short discount books can be increased, or shipping charges added, higher than actual postage. If operating profit is not acceptable, fees should be tested and, if successful, imposed.

MONEY USAGE AND CASH FLOW

Profits and cash flow are partners. If too much of the profits are put into nonproductive or inactive assets, the cash flow dries up, possibly resulting in a period when bills cannot be paid, and reorders and other needs are held up. All merchants should have a clear idea of how much money will be available in future periods to pay for merchandise, operating expenses, and capital improvements and equipment.

Writing a Cash Flow Plan

A simple cash flow projection can be made for six to eight months that will provide a reasonable estimate of how much cash will be available at the end of each month. A written plan can help prevent bill-paying problems and keep inventory and expenses under control. Companies large and small run into trouble, and even fail, because of poor cash flow. Total assets might be greater than total liabilities, but cash cannot be generated fast enough to pay bills. The formula for planning is:

Cash Flow = Cash on Hand at Beginning of Period +
Cash Taken in from All Sources – Cash Payments
for All Reasons during the Period

The following is an example of a six-month cash flow plan, starting on July 1 with $2,000 cash on hand. The plan is made using the prior year's history as a guide. If there is no history, the owner should be very conservative in the use of start-up money.

	July	Aug.	Sept.	Oct.	Nov.	Dec.	Total
July 1 Cash on Hand 2,000 (plus)							
Cash Sales (plus)	$12,000	$12,000	$13,000	$13,000	$15,000	$26,000	$91,000
Accounts Receivable, Cash In (minus)	+3,000	2,000	3,000	4,000	4,000	10,000	26,000
Operating Expenses, Cash Out (minus)	– 5,000	4,900	5,200	5,350	5,900	7,000	33,350
Accounts Payable, Cash Out (minus)	– 9,900	9,380	10,400	11,050	12,350	22,970	76,050
Capital Expenses, Cash Out	– 0	600	0	0	200	0	800
Monthly Totals	+ 100	– 880	+ 400	+ 600	+ 550	+ 6,030	+ 6,800
E.O.M Totals	2,100	1,220	1,620	2,220	2,770	8,800	8,800

NOTE: Cash on hand each month and on December 31 includes the $2,000 available on July 1, and can be used to pay the usual high bills in January.

Accounts Payable

I am often asked what a reasonable accounts payable balance should be. The answer is related to the total cost of inventory on hand. If a bookseller has good cash flow, cash discount terms should be taken for timely payments. If the bookseller wants to build a good credit reputation, all bills should be paid as directed by the suppliers. Both these routines would probably leave an accounts payable balance of between 20 and 30 percent of the cost inventory on hand.

It is important to understand that paying all bills within days after receiving them means releasing money that could be earning interest in certificate accounts. And although publishers become annoyed when accounts habitually pay up after 90 days, they generally do not bother them if history shows that these slow payers are reliable and there are no other credit adjustment problems with them. Not being able to pay bills within 100 to 120 days, however, can be a sign of serious problems, and it is a danger signal if the accounts payable balance is always about 50 percent or more of stock on hand.

Accounts Receivable

Bear in mind that accounts receivables are for collecting. I do not recommend that bookshops, especially new stores, offer personal charge accounts. Most customers have bank credit cards of one kind or another, and accepting them will cost the bookstore less than establishing its own credit and collection department.

If you do offer personal charge accounts, there should be a formal procedure for securing payments on time—one that eliminates bad debts and keeps slow-paying customers to a minimum. Many booksellers are too informal and lax with these accounts. The bills and reminder statements should be businesslike and should be mailed on a definite schedule. A late-payment fee should be considered beyond a reasonable time limit. Do not sit on your customers' accounts—manage them.

Impediments to Cash Flow

It is usually a mistake to open a bookstore with inadequate capital—money that is needed to help the business through its first months, and even years, of getting on its feet. But it is even more of a cardinal sin to withdraw money from cash flow and profits that might be needed to keep an enterprise healthy and growing. A business is not for milking. I have seen stores in jeopardy, and even fail, because the owners paid themselves more than was justified by the financial results. Consequently, they did not have enough cash to reorder needed inventory, replace vital equipment, or to spend on usual expenses, which they were then forced to reduce. Even with a very profitable bookstore business, the owner should carefully consider how much of the net profits should be withdrawn—and, even then, rarely should all of them be withdrawn.

Improving Cash Flow

Too much inventory and high fixed expenses are the main reasons why booksellers have ready-cash problems. There are ways to loosen the money flow fairly quickly:

(1) Plan cash flow for the next few months by charting the expected incoming and outgoing monies.

(2) Be more conservative in new and backlist order quantities.

(3) Make an extra inspection of inventory to return dead and overstock titles.

(4) Analyze all controllable expenses for possible savings.

(5) Review accounts receivable for payments due.

(6) Consider fees to charge for special customer services.

(7) Slow down payments to suppliers if the total is not over 30 percent of cost inventory on hand.

(8) Delay purchases of new equipment, and consider leasing instead of buying.

(9) Run a "cash sale" event as a store promotion.

(10) Apply for a temporary loan to carry the store through a difficult period.

BOOKKEEPING

Because good financial record keeping is so important, I advise bookstores to make up their own stock purchase and receiving records. Keep the method simple and easy to use—and keep it up to date. Be sure these steps are followed:

(1) Check and record all incoming merchandise. If there is a shortage or overage, have a form to record it, and attach it to the packing list or invoice.

(2) On returns to suppliers for any reason, have a chargeback form to record the shipment, enclosing one copy and sending two copies to the office desk, as you do with receivings.

(3) Adjust your next payment to a vendor with the notes of receivings, returns, and mistakes. Why wait for adjustments to come from publishers months later? Why not reduce payments to them yourself and use the money for other needs? Having accurate records on hand will provide fast answers for the suppliers and yourself.

(4) All transactions involving a particular supplier should be filed together and readily available.

Calculating Net Profit

The precision of a store's recorded inventory affects the bookseller's calculation of net profit, on which the annual income tax owed by the business is computed. Even meticulous bookkeeping records do not do the whole job. Physical inventory counts will provide management with evidence of a shortage (or infrequent overage) problem. An accurate physical count also more precisely determines the cost of goods sold and the net profit figure. If the bookstore does not keep track of markdowns and markups when taken, they will be part of the physical count totals.

The following chart shows the difference in the net profit result when two diverse methods are used for the same store operation. One system uses accurate cost of sales, with actual

beginning and ending physical inventory counts and valid purchase figures. The second method estimates cost of goods sold
by using an assumed gross margin figure of 38.5%, when not
keeping track of actual cost of books, transportation, and price
changes.

	Physical Inventory		Assumed Gross Margin	
	$	%	$	%
Sales	300,000	100.0	300,000	100.0
Cost of Sales				
Beginning Inventory	176,000			
Purchases	177,000			
Total	253,000			
Ending Inventory	61,000			
Cost of Goods Sold	192,000	64.0	184,500	61.5
Gross Profit	108,000	36.0	115,500	38.5
Operating Expenses	96,900	32.3	96,900	32.3
Net Profit	11,100	3.7	18,600	6.2

NOTE: It is evident in the latter procedure that management does not know
that $7,500, 2.5% of sales, is lost in shortage and in price changes taken,
resulting in excessive tax payments on the inaccurate net profit.

BOOKSTORE WORTH

Let's say a bookshop owner, after being in business a few years,
realizes that the return on investment is not up to expectations.
Whether intending to sell or not, the owner should have an idea
of the worth of the business—for estate planning purposes, to
obtain a loan, or to sell quickly if necessary. A store's worth
consists mainly of two components: (1) solid assets, or today's
replacement or depreciated value of inventory, fixtures, equipment, and the like; and (2) profitability, which determines
"goodwill" value by analyzing current profit and the effect on
future profitability of sales trends, the market, the industry, and
competition. If trends are favorable, goodwill could amount to
two to four times current profit. If it has been a break-even or

unprofitable business, there may be no goodwill. Two stores with the same sales volume could have very different worths.

A careful analysis of the balance sheet and other financial statements will determine the solvency of a business. Steady operating profits each year usually mean a successful business. The balance sheet, only looked at superficially by many merchants, gives many clues to the soundness of the bookstore operation:

(1) *Cash and Other Money Assets*—if all liabilities and loans are being paid off on time, continual plus balances are a good sign.

(2) *Inventory on Hand*—this figure, in relation to sales and desired turnover, will tell the owner whether or not the merchandise is being managed well.

(3) *Accounts Payable*—if the balance owed to merchandise suppliers is less than 40 percent of the inventory on hand at cost, it is a favorable sign.

(4) *Notes Payable*—if borrowings are not being reduced, it could be a bad sign.

(5) *Current Ratio* $= \dfrac{\text{Current Assets}}{\text{Current Liabilities}}$

If the ratio is more than one, preferably close to two, the business should be in good condition.

(6) *Working Capital* = Current Assets – Current Liabilities shows the cash worth of assets left over if all current liabilities were paid off; the balance can be used for other needs.

SUMMARY

Booksellers are advised to plan their finances wisely and to seek counsel from experts. ABA's education department offers financial seminars from time to time that address these issues. Budget, operating expense, cost of sales, money handling, and bookkeeping are pressure points a bookseller should monitor to gauge the financial health of the business. Prevention is the best medicine, and booksellers who are ever alert to all the symptoms of financial problems can best remedy the situation before a crisis occurs—maintaining the store's sound financial condition.

5

Personnel Management

I t cannot be overemphasized that the success of a bookstore often turns on the abilities and attitudes of the staff. Good working conditions and effective supervision are the keys to a satisfied and productive workforce. Maintaining a superior staff, however, requires constant effort, teaching, and encouragement. In this section I offer tips that should make personnel management a little easier for the bookseller.

THE INTERVIEW PROCESS

Interviewing prospective employees is an important part of building a reliable, resourceful staff. Before a job interview begins, the bookseller should request a complete job application or resume. This can help guide the interview—showing possible conflicting statements, listing educational and employment background, and even giving hints of the applicant's attitude, personality, and general qualifications.

In the interview, the applicant's demeanor should be scrutinized by the prospective employer to determine the potential employee's physical energy, desire to do a good job, willingness to work with other staff members and customers in a pleasant way, truthfulness, and possible harmful prejudices. Be on the lookout for critical statements about former employers.

Overqualified applicants should not be considered if your bookshop lacks opportunities for promotion, causing possible quick departures from jobs. *Do* be up front about the future. The applicant should be honestly apprised of potential compensation growth, based on merit and promotions. The employee should not be left to discover one or two years down the road that the bookstore can only afford minimum increases in compensation, if any, or that there is no room to take on upgraded duties.

Remember to check references. No matter how little a former employer might be willing to say, it is important to get an impression of satisfaction with the work done at a previous job. Some clue to the prospect's habits and abilities might come out in a short conversation, and try to obtain a "yes" or "no" answer to the question "would you rehire this person?" Although some companies now have a policy against providing references, at the least you can confirm that the employee actually worked there and the dates of employment.

An important caveat should be added to this section. The laws and regulations governing hiring are complex. Before interviewing, be aware of what questions you are legally entitled to ask and what factors you may or may not consider in refusing employment to an applicant.

JOB TRAINING

Always provide and discuss a written job description, both at the interview and when the employee begins work. Employee turnover is often the result of new workers not knowing what is expected of them, only to find themselves with duties not to their liking or that they cannot perform adequately. Below is a simple list of responsibilities usually performed by bookshop employees. (Tasks can be added or deleted to fit the needs of particular stores.) It is imperative that each function be explained and understood by each worker:

• sell books, with proper customer service, courtesy, and a good attitude;

• bring customers to the requested title location as often as possible and offer service;

• try to make a suggestion sale, or extra sale, especially when you know a customer's category of interest;

• make no promises to customers, but make every effort to satisfy their purchase aims;

• ask another staff member for help when you do not have an answer or cannot satisfy a customer;

• answer and help telephone customers as if they were in the store, and offer to call back with information not readily available;

• learn the location of all subjects and titles and incoming books as much as possible;

• know how to use the tools of the trade, such as *Books in Print* and the *ABA Book Buyer's Handbook*;

• gain merchandise knowledge by checking book highlights, new titles, and book jackets as time allows;

• be skilled at register checkout: handling customers' purchases, cash versus charge, credits and refunds, money handling and movement;

• learn receiving/shipping room duties, including opening, checking in, and pricing of incoming stock;

• help in arranging and promoting books in window and floor displays;

• know how to process returns: finding, checking, packing, and recording overstocks;

• take part in any stock control procedures;

• pass on any information that will help the buyer have the right books, at the right time, in the right quantities;

• be alert to customer actions and movements to help protect the money and merchandise assets of the store;

• be flexible and willing to cooperate with management at all times;

• be willing to help in all housekeeping duties, including shelf cleaning and rest room chores;
   • arrive at work on time and know your schedule in advance;
   • present a good appearance and behave appropriately; and
   • get along with other employees and work with them when necessary.

An important axiom is that you should not hire a person to perform only one job. Most stores do not need, nor can they afford, specialists. The smaller the staff, the more important for all employees to know how to handle most bookshop tasks. Selling, stock work, displaying, receiving and shipping, and cashiering are jobs that can be handled by all staff members. Bookstores suffer from poor productivity when individuals are not proficient in all of these work areas. Only high-volume stores, with perhaps 10 or more employees, are designed to have specialists who handle just checkout work or receiving.

PERSONNEL MANAGEMENT

Once staff members are hired and trained, it is important for booksellers to work at keeping them. Be sure to teach your employees all you know about how to run a bookshop. Stimulate them by letting them take on as many managing duties as possible. Listen to their ideas on how to improve operations. Above all, take the time to compliment workers who do a good job. Too often management is quick to criticize but slow to express approval of employee actions. I have found praise to be the most useful tool to attain better performance and to retain superior staff members.

One detail that contributes to a smoothly run staff is a written work schedule; this is especially necessary for larger stores. Work hours should be assigned according to the needs of the bookstore for each week and posted before the end of the previous week. There should be no room for an excuse like "I didn't know I was due here this morning."

Three main factors determine when certain employees should be on duty—basic coverage for managing and operating the store, peak traffic and sales times, and heavy stock workload times. When employees are hired, they should know their work schedule by days and hours—subject to occasional adjustments to fit the needs of the bookstore and the convenience of the worker. Employees should not switch hours with co-workers without the approval of the manager. Such changes can result in too many overtime hours, the receiving room getting behind schedule, haphazard merchandise displays, and lack of customer service—all the problems a well thought-out schedule strives to avoid.

Staff meetings may be a helpful management tool. Some employees and management people find it easier to relax in a group and open up with questions and thoughts they hold back in one-on-one discussions. Use these meetings to communicate management plans, ideas, and goals while getting feedback from workers. Be sure to keep the meetings well planned, short, and simple.

Managing personnel also demands some general housekeeping duties, aside from scheduling and payroll. Keep a written file for each employee. Good and poor work habits should be noted and discussed in detail periodically with each employee, with a record of the talk dated and initialed by both parties. It is especially important that discussions leading up to possible future dismissal be documented to avoid potential charges of wrongful and unlawful discharges.

It goes without saying that one of the toughest jobs for a bookstore manager is firing an employee. It is not a simple task, and it can be emotional; but it has to be done once in a while, and it should not be delegated. The manager should be armed with the facts warranting dismissal, while considering the potential feelings and reaction of the employee. The task may be made easier if the termination is not a complete surprise. The reasons for the decision should have been discussed thoroughly two or more times before, to serve as warnings. Refer to notes, dated and signed, in the worker's personnel file. Well-kept records will also discourage discharged workers from acting in a damaging fashion toward their former employer and preclude labor department intervention. Again, it is important to be aware of relevant employment law. The employer should be fastidious in documenting the steps leading to termination in the event the worker decides to challenge the discharge.

PAYROLL EXPENSES

As discussed previously, payroll may account for 40 to 50 percent of total operating expenses, making payroll the largest controllable expense in a store's operation. Total other expenses are a governing factor, suggesting a tighter or looser payroll, as well as the bookshop owner's philosophy regarding customer service in terms of desired staff size. The demographics of the market should be considered when deciding what kind of service to provide to ensure a good balance between service and sales without a negative effect on profit.

When hiring, keep part-time help in mind. In my early management years, I believed that it was very important to have as much continuity of an employee's work time as possible to build knowledge of inventory availability and movement. I soon learned, however, that part-time staffers can keep labor costs down and be an invaluable resource—assisting the store during busy selling periods, handling receiving backlogs, and even filling in when regular staff members do not show up for work. The larger the bookstore volume, the more crucial to have regular and on-call part-time employees. Small personal bookshops aside, a staff solely composed of full-time workers may mean low productivity at times, causing a too-high payroll to sales ratio.

Booksellers must be careful to consider state and federal labor laws while cutting payroll expenses. Take three examples

I have encountered in the past: one bookstore did not pay an employee one-and-one-half times her regular rate of pay for hours worked over 40 per week; another bookshop paid the federal minimum wage instead of the state minimum, which was higher; a third store did not pay workers for required attendance at staff meetings, held after store closing. These stores not only had to compensate their help when it was brought to the attention of local labor boards, but also had to pay penalties to the state. Knowing the law ahead of time can save a bookseller much grief and dollars.

PRODUCTIVITY EXPECTATIONS

Productivity is the secret to a regulated payroll, and as book prices have increased in recent years, higher sales per employee should be achieved. From my experience, I offer the following ranges, based on a 40-hour work week, as a very general guide to employee productivity expectations in various sales volume categories:

Sales to $100,000	. . . . .	$50,000 to $70,000
250,000	. . . . .	55,000 to 75,000
400,000	. . . . .	60,000 to 80,000
600,000	. . . . .	65,000 to 85,000

In larger volume operations, perhaps another 40 hours' work might be scheduled for each $100,000 sales increase. Also keep in mind that if the pay scale in an area is high, it may be necessary to schedule fewer work hours. And, as discussed, using part-time help can also improve productivity by eliminating work hours in slow selling periods.

SUMMARY

Let me wrap up this section on personnel by reminding booksellers that payroll is usually a bookstore's largest operating expense; careful consideration should therefore be given to the proper size and kind of staff a particular bookstore needs. Also keep in mind that not only do efficient employees save the store money; courteous, knowledgeable workers keep customers coming back.

6

Security in the Bookstore

I find it astonishing that some bookstores do not take even basic security measures to safeguard their assets. While poor bookkeeping and record procedures are often used to explain shrinkage in bookstores, they are probably less of a factor than theft. Shrinkage, attributable to both customer traffic and staff, can lead to overall increases in the cost of sales. It is therefore essential that managers set up a system to secure the movement of money, merchandise, equipment, and supplies.

The best deterrent to stealing is a staff that is constantly "minding the store"—in other words, paying close attention to everything going on around them. Security should be part of every employee's job description. Written rules concerning the handling of money are helpful. And remember to prevent temptation! Keep the safe locked, inspect the register tapes daily, record all book shipments, do not sign checks without ascertaining that the bill is valid, control cash refunds and credit slips, and maintain a record of books borrowed by employees. Every measure taken to reduce shrinkage, no matter how trivial, will have an effect on bottom-line profits.

CUSTOMER THEFT

While most booksellers might prefer to give their customers the benefit of the doubt, it is unfortunate but true that shoplifting is some people's chosen profession. Although most shoplifters work alone, there may be teams of them, looking for open safes, packages of books left outside the receiving door, and workers' pocketbooks and wallets. A team member might try to divert the attention of an employee while a partner does the dirty work.

Experienced shoplifters can sometimes be spotted as frequent browsers who never buy a book. One of the best ways to discourage professionals is to greet them as if they are recognized or known. The more familiarization a store employee can project toward suspected potential shoplifters, the better the chance that they will be discouraged from carrying out their plans. It is foolish, however, to rely too heavily on the ability to spot shoplifters based on attire and image—appearances can often be misleading—so it is especially important for employees to be alert at all times.

Other simple measures can be taken to prevent theft. If bar coding is not in use, checkout employees can be trained to make sure that the actual price of each book matches the price ticket. This safeguard would catch much of the price-ticket switching that goes on in bookstores. Using different color price tags for different categories of books might help identify changed tickets, or you might consider using a price sticker that splits into at least two parts when removed. However, a thorough knowledge of merchandise and close scrutiny at the checkout are the best deterrents.

Do not keep the receiving/stock rooms unlocked and the doors open. In my experience, this is one of the major causes of shortage. Professional shoplifters know that money, merchandise, and other valuables are usually placed there (some employees have also been known to take advantage of this dangerous habit). Shipping/stock rooms should be kept locked and, when the need arises, opened by authorized workers only. A bell will allow for deliveries and a safety bar can handle emergency openings. The front door of the store should be used for all employee comings and goings.

Unbelievably, some bookstores actually create thieves. When apprehended, some shoplifters—with no record of past stealing—have admitted that they stole a book only because of the employees. Socializing staff members, ignoring those customers' needs, angered them to the point where they "got even" by stealing books. Workers should be attentive, available, and willing to help. An alert image will reduce the number of vengeful customers, while deterring regular shoplifters. And, remember, getting away with stealing once will encourage further attempts.

EMPLOYEE THEFT

Most employees are honest, but there is a minority of staff members who cannot resist taking easily available funds. The bigger the bookstore and the more people employed, the greater the chances of missing funds. Anyone, from an old-time manager to the newest employee, may be involved. Theft by an employee is sometimes motivated by sloppy money handling or poor cash control. Prevention of opportunities is one of the best ways to protect money and other assets, causing fewer people to feel the urge to steal. Large amounts of money should not be left to accumulate in cash registers. Sales receipts should be deposited daily at the bank and not be left to collect for a few days, even in a locked safe. Weekend and holiday receipts should be brought to a bank depository whenever possible.

A cash register cannot talk, but careful analysis of the register tape can tell a bookseller quite a lot about the movement of money in his or her store. The register should have a running tape that is removed and checked daily. Each customer should receive a receipt and, most important, every "void" or "no sale" slip should to be marked with the reason, initialed, and placed in the cash drawer. Always check the register tape's detail numbers. I remember one instance where analysis of the last receipt numbers at night and the first ring the next day disclosed a discrepancy. Further investigation brought an admission from an employee that he sometimes closed out the register one hour before store closing, took the money on sales made that last hour, and then put in a new tape for the next day, with no thought of receipt numbers. Register tapes are an important money control.

A loosely monitored cash register is not the only inducement to employee theft. Keep a close watch on the shipping/receiving room and be alert to a large number of reported shortages on shipments from publishers. An employee can easily spread such shortages around among the hundreds of suppliers used by the bookshop—in the meantime taking the books home. Bear in mind that the accounting office is a security area too. The keepers of financial records have the opportunity to alter, and even to create, accounts from which to siphon off funds. The store owner should read and analyze all financial statements and question any unfamiliar and unusual items and accounts. Back-up evidence should be attached to a copy of each check to be scrutinized and then signed by the owner or a knowledgeable delegate.

Be on the lookout for any oddities in an employee's work schedule. Question why a staff member shows up often when not scheduled to work, or why he or she is always volunteering to work nights and weekends or other times when the owner might not be present. All employees should be required to use vacation time, days off, and other scheduled absences; it is surprising what might be discovered when someone else takes over their tasks. Of course, it is important to restate that most bookshop personnel are honest—but it doesn't hurt to be alert.

SUMMARY

One of the most important duties of all those who work in a bookstore is to protect the assets of the business. Store security must be a concerted effort between management and personnel aimed at detecting and preventing theft. Constant vigilance is the best form of detection, and the absence of temptation the best form of prevention. In the long run, reducing shrinkage lowers the cost of sales and has a positive effect on bottom-line profits.

7

Promoting Your Store and Your Merchandise

P romotion is any and every action taken to sell more of a product. Bookstore promotion can include advertising, in-store merchandising, creative pricing, special events, and publicity. Each of these techniques serves a different function, but all ultimately aim to accomplish one thing—selling more books.

Advertising is paid promotion, offering merchandise for sale or announcing a special event. It is usually directed to the stores' market via the local media—newspapers, radio, and TV—or through direct mail pieces such as catalogs, letters, and package stuffers. Another form of bookshop advertising is done in cooperation with publishers, who pay a certain part of the cost. In-store merchandising is point-of-purchase promotion, boosting individual titles and categories of books in a manner to attract attention and create sales. Creative pricing projects an image of savings that allows general bookstores to compete with their discount competition. Special events may include book fairs, author autographing parties, and sidewalk sales. Publicity is free promotion.

ADVERTISING

The Advertising Budget

The experts say that to be successful, advertising should be continuous, consistent, and repetitious. But because of the small gross profit margin in bookselling, booksellers are generally reluctant to spend the four, six, even ten percent of sales that other merchants spend for promotion. I recommend that the general trade bookshop budget one-and-one-half to two-and-one-half percent of sales for advertising. (The budget is composed of net dollars to be spent, after rebates from cooperating publishers.) In the small- to medium-sized store, a good part of that budget will go for promoting the store's location, services, and a mix of merchandise in the classified telephone directory and other local media. The greater the volume, the larger the share of the budget that can be allotted for book promotion. Sending direct mail promotions to a select, category-related group of customers is also helpful at certain times of the year and might be included in the basic budget.

Does it pay to advertise specific titles? Some booksellers say yes and some say no. I believe that it does pay most of the time because the publishers pay a substantial part of the cost. No doubt many dollars are wasted when an ad is not well planned, or if it is produced needlessly, merely because the resource money is available. But when the right book or group of titles are publicized at the right time, in the right place, it can be productive for both the bookseller and the publisher.

I have always found that bargain books are the most productive category to advertise. Whether in newspapers or by direct mail, the announcement of savings usually produces the most store traffic and sales and brings in more mail orders. New, well-chosen nonfiction titles usually create adequate sales, especially if they are reference-type works. It is with new fiction books that selectivity is important; stick with well-known, established authors. Much ad money is wasted on the great expectations of up-and-coming authors. Proven, seasonal backlist titles can be advertised advantageously at the right time. But whatever books are promoted, the cooperation of the publishers should be sought.

Plan to boost the bookshop's name and store highlights when the potential for creating extra sales is highest. Some booksellers budget and spend ad dollars evenly, month by month. Expected store traffic and sales are not the same every month, however, and booksellers ought to take advantage of the best traffic and customer buying needs. The largest amount of advertising dollars should be spent just before and during peak holiday buying (November, December), June and other giftgiving months, school openings, and other seasonal special occasions.

Co-op Advertising

It is surprising how many booksellers do not seek publishers' help when planning their advertising. Almost any bookshop, no matter how small its sales volume, can earn co-op advertising money. Even small rebates averaging $15 each from 20 suppliers during the year total $300 extra profit. It takes almost $10,000 in sales for the average bookstore to earn $300 bottom-line profit. It is important to be familiar with publishers' co-op advertising policies (many of these are listed in the *ABA Book Buyer's Handbook*); when in doubt, contact the publisher before planning your promotion to ensure that you understand the conditions that must be met to get your co-op money.

Print Ads

Classified telephone directory advertising is a must for bookstores, but the size and cost of the ad should be kept within reason. An oversized, first-year message might be acceptable to draw attention to the new store; in following years, however, the ad should be examined in line with its productivity and the expense dollars available. A maturing bookstore might not need the biggest ad in the yellow pages.

Take advantage of your ad space, wherever possible, by including an order form. It is easier for customers to fill out a form than to travel to a bookstore. Whether the ad appears in a newspaper, envelope stuffer, or catalog, a simple order coupon should be part of it; if there is more than one title being promoted, number them on the coupon so that customers can circle the numbers of the books being ordered. Allowing books to be charged to a credit card is another incentive that attracts orders. When advertising several books, try to include one or two low-priced or reduced-price titles. Often, one of these will catch the eye of the reader who has just about decided to skip the order.

Learn to say no occasionally to "institutional" advertising that is akin to donation expense. Some merchants find it difficult to turn away requests for ads in local school and church tabloids, miscellaneous programs and announcements, and local bulletins and periodicals of all kinds. Booksellers may feel that although there may not be a measurable sales return, this is important as goodwill advertising. If you decide to do some institutional advertising, make an effort to skip some publications and eliminate consecutive appearances in others.

Barter Advertising

Make your bookstore a presence on the local scene by tying in books with neighboring businesses. For example, when a nearby theater is showing a movie based on a classic title or new bestseller, the theater management might allow the bookshop to hang a poster in its lobby in return for the store placing a movie poster in its window. A local travel store might do the same—exchanging travel book news for travel agency publicity. Even displaying some garden tools with garden books in your window display might earn space at the local hardware store for promotion of your garden book selection. There are trade books that can be related to almost any kind of business, special-interest group, club, or local holiday—the tie-in possibilities are unlimited. Best of all, this kind of promotion doesn't cost the bookseller a cent.

Direct Mail

Another approach to advertising, albeit an expensive one, is direct mail. With the continual increase in postal charges, direct mail promotion has to be efficient and timely to attain profitable results. One of the most important factors is how the customer mailing list is made up and monitored. Too many booksellers do not examine the effects of their mailings as compared to the costs. For best returns:

• Mailing lists should be broken down into customer interests.

• The lists should be kept up to date, removing bad addresses, and unfamiliar names should be deleted every 18 to 24 months.

• New names should be added by some routine of extracting names from credit-card charges, special orders, and customers who make large purchases in the store.

• Mailings should be well thought-out and should not be sent haphazardly.

• Make use of bulk-mailing rates whenever possible.

• Give out extra copies of mailing pieces to store customers.

• If possible, use publishers' ready-made promotion pieces, which are usually available at no cost.

• Keep track of costs and estimated direct-mail results.

• Consider a Christmas brochure or catalog as a main mailing piece for the year.

Newsletters serve as a productive avenue for many booksellers. Most of the four- to eight-page specimens I have read are a good blend of institutional and book advertising, interesting personal messages, and soft-sell merchandise promotion. The cost of a simple-format newsletter is reasonable, and by using an active customer mailing list, extra sales and customer loyalty are created. Be sure to check with the publishers; some will rebate co-op money for titles included in the newsletter.

Don't fret about publishers' direct promotion of their books to the retail customers or about book-club promotions. The more they spend on promotion, the more sales the bookshops will gain in the end. Most people receiving book-related direct mail end up going to their bookstore for the titles. Book clubs have a large membership turnover, and when their members' subscriptions expire they turn to bookstores.

IN-STORE MERCHANDISING

A key element of promotion is the process of arranging and displaying merchandise in the store. It is a way of addressing the customers, asking their eyes to look at what you have and stopping their feet from passing by. A display may remind a customer of his or her interest in the merchandise or even create a desire for it. Visual selling is very important in these days of self-service and self-selection, and it is also a way to help customers find the books they seek.

Where to Put What

When a bookseller is thinking about how to arrange an interior display, the various areas of the bookstore should be considered as they relate to customer movement. The front section of the store draws more people than the middle section, which in turn draws more than the back. The entrance and checkout areas have a greater number of passersby than ends of tables and gondolas, which draw more people than shelf displays. Therefore, bestsellers and new titles expected to be good sellers should occupy flat display spaces in the highest traffic areas to create the most potential for impulse purchases. Pay particular attention to the checkout area when promoting books. It is the most trafficked area in the store. Some merchants put deadwood there hoping to move a copy or two, but the space would be better used to generate impulse buys. Good sellers, promising new titles, and novelty books, especially low-priced ones, are often added to a customer's purchases while at the cash counter. I know of one veteran bookseller who placed humor, basic, and theme titles there and found that more copies were sold at the checkout than at their usual location in the store.

More potential customers see books in window displays than the same amount of stock anywhere else in the store. Use this fact to draw people in. Window displays should be simple and attractive, showing as many titles as possible of a single theme or a few different categories. Use signs with selling words that explain the display, the bookstore's inventory, or special events. I don't believe in having lots of non-book merchandise in the window as props, even though it may relate to the books. More books in the window results in increased sales.

Flat displays attract more eyes. The full cover of a book will get more notice than if only the spine is displayed. Every space advantage should be seized to merchandise book jackets, whether on tables, shelves, or special fixtures. For a small store, when ten, five, or even three copies come into stock, the book is probably expected to be a good seller, and a flat space should be made for this important title. As a rule, three copies flat on a shelf, one behind the other, will beckon to the customer more than five spine-displayed copies next to each other. Be sure to pyramid table displays. Many titles laid out side by side and face up will look like one big picture blur. There should be one or two large quantity highlights in or near the middle of the table, with other titles in various quantities sloping away to the four sides. Different heights will help frame each title, attracting attention to the various books. Boxes wrapped in gift paper can add height to small quantities.

Try to display paperback and hardcover books together. Although one shelf may be lost in some sections because of the varying heights of some formats, it will be made up by other space savings. Very often, two paperback and two hardbound sections of a category fit well into three sections when combined—it is easier to place books when copies arrive in stock, and it is a service to customers to have all books on a subject, or by an author, in one place.

A bookstore's image of having a great selection of books is enhanced when fixtures and bare spaces are covered with merchandise and signs. Every attempt should be made to hide empty spaces with the inventory on hand, rather than waiting for more books to come in. If it is obvious that there is too much room for the sales potential, closing off some of the store space should be considered.

Never waste valuable display space on deadwood. I once approached a branch store and saw a prominent window exhibit of a title six-months old, which I knew was a dud. Inside the doorway was another flat display of the book. When I questioned the manager, he answered that before returning the books he was trying to sell some copies. His reasoning was mistaken—deadwood is precisely that because it will not sell. Instead, display the best or most recent books in front of people's eyes. Theoretically, the number-one bestseller or expected to be bestseller should be placed in the number-one impulse spot, the number two in the number-two spot, and on down the line. Of course, it is impossible to stick to this axiom with all displays; but at least the top one to two percent of titles should occupy the best space.

Visual Displays

Sometimes stores provide a wide selection of books, have adequate personnel and services available, and are located in fairly good places, yet the businesses do not grow. Lack of pizzazz in merchandising could be the reason. A merchandise presentation that looks tired, stale, and uninteresting will not draw customers into the store. Booksellers should take the following steps to convey an impression of excitement:

• Rearrange and change book displays often, even moving categories once in a while.

• Use more color on sections of bare walls and fixtures, using posters or paint, for example, to brighten the area.

• Use more explicit and colorful signage within the store and in the windows, with stimulating wording.

• Put a bargain book table display at the front of the store.

• Hang banners occasionally that will flaunt your offerings, services, and values.

• Promote special events such as "Book of the Week," "Manager's Sale," or "Dollar Days."

• Create more special theme displays throughout the year that tie in with holidays, local events, author appearances, TV and movie specials, travel, gardening, and school-opening times.

Visual selling aids are very important when trying to create impulse purchases of bargain books. When looking at general trade books, customers usually search out one or two subject areas, with definite titles or themes in mind. But at the bargain displays, browsers will examine all kinds of books. Enticing signs and a table display near the front of the store are the best ways to merchandise bargain books. Use the two-price gimmick and show both the original and sale price. This way the amount of savings is noticed quickly by shoppers, and it very often leads to extra sales. Remember, everyone loves a bargain.

Signage is an adjunct to displays, helping to focus the customers' attention on particular books or categories. In addition to being a directional tool, a good sign that contains descriptive, selling words can create in a browser a desire to make a purchase of the title on display. Tables, walls, and gondolas should have some signage to tell browsers what they contain. Very large categories, such as children's books and bargain books, should have hanging signs to attract and inform customers. Keep in mind that the new generations of book customers, who have grown up in an atmosphere of self-service, often will not look for a salesperson if they do not find the books they want.

So you usually throw out all those posters you get in the mail? Like good signs, posters are seen and read by a large number of customers. They highlight important books and promote an interest in them. Posters help build good displays in the store and in windows. Booksellers can make their own posters by cutting out reviews, publishers' ads, and even the ads of competitive stores and placing them on boards, adding copy with colored markers. Book jackets are also useful in making posters. Avoid the impulse to discard posters before thinking how they might be used.

Good displays are worth repeating. Repetition of successful advertising and promotion is a principle of retailing, and that includes merchandise display. Whether it is gardening or travel books in the spring, reference books for school opening, or a tie-in with some local event, displays create excitement and many customers look forward to the same category or theme of titles periodically. Displaying the right books at appropriate times also reminds browsers that they should be thinking of buying those titles now.

CREATIVE PRICING

I have found that many prospective booksellers worry about opening their shops near discount bookstores. My answering thoughts always revolve around selection, pricing, service, and convenience. In general, the greater the distance between stores, the less the effect on the conventionally priced shop. The closer you are, the greater the savings image that must be projected to combat discounting. Creative pricing could be a solution. The best service and convenience rarely beat selection and pricing, but we should not close our eyes to the fact that some discounters offer a wide selection of titles. There are numerous cases where independent booksellers, and even branches of chain stores, have closed because they did not offer a significantly better stock selection than their discount competition.

Many booksellers miss out on sizable sales and an opportunity to present themselves as having "discounts," because they do not take advantage of the market for bargain books. These include remainders, reprints, special buys, imports, and hurt books. Some bookshop buyers just dabble in this area, trying out some every once in a while in the store. If there is space for them, a good assortment of bargain books should always be on hand, taking up from five to ten percent of the selling space of a general bookshop. These books are profitable, easy to control, and they stimulate and enhance the value image of the bookstore. In these days of growing discounting, promoting bargains is a way to retain regular customers and gain new ones.

Multiple pricing can move books faster and produce extra sales. It is especially helpful when a store has lots of miscellaneous markdowns. "Three for $5" is better than $1.75 each, and "59¢ each or two for $1" will move books faster than 50¢ each. Advertise a hardbound dictionary and thesaurus at a discount if bought as a set. And why not give away a box of pencils with every dictionary or crossword book? There are plenty of opportunities to be creative in pricing while expanding the savings image.

I have often wondered why more booksellers do not take advantage of the coupon-clipping habits of millions of shoppers. Customers look forward to the special newspaper editions and other publications that contain money-saving coupons on food and hundreds of other household products. Merchants who promote items in this way talk of the increased sales made via coupon advertising. Even though books are not strictly necessities of life, promoting the right titles at the right times with coupons might be a creative way to increase sales while combating discount competition.

SPECIAL EVENTS

Promoting books through special events shows customers that something new and different is happening at the bookstore. It is a way to expand sales by attracting new customers, sometimes with the bookseller bringing books to potential customers, rather than bringing customers to the store. Out-of-store events could relate to literary workshops, local conferences, author luncheons, or school book fairs. Holidays, charity occasions, current events, seasonal or regional themes, or the store's anniversary might be celebrated by book readings and author parties and sidewalk and other sales, for example. The variety of special events possible is limited only by the ingenuity of the bookseller.

PUBLICITY

Publicity is one of the most desirable forms of advertising, because it's free. It is important to let the local media know what's going on in your bookstore. The news media are always on the lookout for interesting items to fill news columns and air time. When you schedule a special event, be sure to send out a press release; make it short, emphasizing the exciting points. Items of interest might include charitable promotions, store anniversaries, children's and school events, and especially author signings. For author signings, let the press know well in advance who's coming to your store, when, and why this will be of interest to readers or viewers. You can usually get photographs from the publisher to send out with your release. If the press picks up on the story before the event, participation will surely grow. Even if no pre-occasion publicity appears, try to get the media to come to your event. Any mention of the event, even if it's too late to increase attendance, will make more people aware of your store and the role it plays in the community.

SUMMARY

Whatever form of promotion is used, each project should be evaluated so that the bookseller can make knowledgeable decisions about advertising specific titles or categories of books in the future, or the effectiveness of various advertising media. Sales made after the advertising or promotion occurs should be compared with past sales. Staff members, knowing what titles are being publicized, should ask customers buying the books if they saw the promotion. An increase in mail and telephone orders can be a clue to money well spent. Immediate monetary results are not the only factor used to measure advertising success, however. A well-developed promotional campaign that keeps the store's name and stock selection in the minds of potential customers will generate more book sales over time.

8

Growing a Healthy Business

Bookselling, perhaps more than any other category of retailing, is a small volume per store business in an industry requiring constant supervision of details. The majority of bookstores, which average under $300,000 in annual sales volume, are especially vulnerable to the downward trends of business cycles. Entrepreneurs and managers can maximize their chances of success by being aggressive, by skilled planning and follow-through, by possessing good merchandising sense, and by canny selection and supervision. Drawing from lessons learned in retailing, what follows is a synopsis of factors that determine a bookstore's ability to prosper.

LOCATION

A good location, chosen after the owner has thoroughly analyzed the business area and book market, can provide the bookseller with a large potential clientele and a receptive market. Location can be "the kiss of death" for many reasons, however, including an insufficient market for books in the area, a deteriorating business and/or residential region, or costly rent for the sales volume achievable in that location.

AVAILABILITY

One of the best ways to build a thriving bookstore and a loyal clientele is to stock the widest and best selection in the area. This is particularly important in the bookstore business, since often there is no substitute for a wanted title. Availability of selection by subject also creates extra sales; book lovers enjoy browsing in stores that offer a diverse assortment of books in their areas of interest, so there is an increase in profitable impulse sales. Inadequate or questionable title assortments and chronic out-of-stock situations can lose potential sales and engender overall dissatisfaction with your store.

STOCK CONTROL

The speed of movement of books into and out of the store is one barometer used to measure the health of the business. The higher the turnover, the better the return on money invested. The same money can be used over again, instead of requiring additional money to buy more books. The regular removal of deadwood is part of efficient turnover. Weak markdown and return procedures can cause the loss of potential sales by cluttering up shelves with unsalable books. The buyer who does not understand the formula of inventory in relation to sales and purchases and cannot judge the speed of sale of individual titles, either from records or observation, could be causing the store to fail.

KNOWING THE MARKET

Effective booksellers research the demographics of their area. Population mix, income, age, and education all provide clues that enable the bookseller to match the store's merchandise and image to the market. Become familiar with the local library's collection and ask customers why they are ordering or requesting titles not usually stocked. It goes without saying that shoppers will frequent the store that carries the merchandise they want.

CUSTOMER SERVICE

One can run a clean, convenient, well-stocked bookstore and still miss out on a segment of the market because of poor or unrealistic customer service policies. Many people will not shop in a store where they have difficulty returning a wrong selection, for example, and where they may have to face questioning or unpleasantness. Good customer service and selling practices are important elements in gaining customer loyalty. Bookstore employees should always keep in mind that customer purchases pay their salaries, and that customers should always leave the bookshop happy. The bookstore that does create an image of courteous, friendly service has a great advantage over the competition that doesn't.

COMPETITION

It is important to realize that the opening of a competing bookstore in the area does not demand the demise of an existing store. It does mean, however, that a new situation has developed, and the first owner must work harder to retain customers and attract new ones. In the past, as bookselling chains grew and discount bookstores proliferated, some traditional bookstores went out of business. No doubt some stores simply could not hold off the formidable competition of the big fellows. But others could have maintained profitability and stayed healthy by analyzing the situation and making some adjustments to their own book operations. Some did make such changes and remained successful by learning to be better managers. It is not easy to offset the strong competition of big, growing companies, but it can be done.

FINANCIAL MANAGEMENT

Two main reasons for the financial success of bookstores are good inventory control and good operating-expense control. Making and monitoring a budget can alert the bookseller to problems, allowing for timely adjustments. Unrealistic sales expectations have put some bookstores in financial binds. If a bookshop is not generating enough cash flow at the right times, available funds must be used for fixed expenses, with not enough left over for buying needed merchandise. Sometimes a store is financially strapped because the owner "milks the cash," taking out too much for personal needs.

RENT

Occupancy costs have a great influence on store profit. A bookseller should first figure the expected annual sales, bearing in mind the amount of space needed to attain that volume, and then calculate a reasonable rent, which should never be more than 10 percent of sales. Since rent is a fixed expense, a high ratio of rent to sales saddles the bookseller with a monthly expense that does not take into account sales' fluctuations. Money that should be available to purchase inventory may have to be used to pay rent, thereby decreasing the store's selection and losing sales, a situation that could cause the store to fold in a recession of any length.

INVESTMENT CAPITAL

Some new bookstores go out of business within months because they do not have enough money to pay their merchandise and operating expenses. Often the new merchant miscalculates projected sales and inventory turnover, or puts too much capital into fixtures and equipment and not enough into salable inventory. It takes time to build customer traffic; enough money is therefore needed to carry the bookstore's expenses for 6 to 12 months.

SECURITY

Shortage is well-recognized as a problem in retailing but few in the profession realize how often it has contributed to store failure. Shrinkage reduces gross margin and operating profit, and all too often it is the largest cost of doing business after payroll and rent. If shortage persists at three to seven percent of sales, compared to an industry average of one to two percent, it could wipe out the bottom-line profit for the period, and the bookstore might not be able to recover.

IMAGE

This factor is not as measurable as some of the others, but it can have a discernible impact on the well-being of the business. Eye-catching displays, friendly service, and a store designed with self-service in mind will attract an increasing number of customers. An offputting image usually results from a gradual deterioration in many areas of store operation, ranging from unexciting or disorganized merchandise displays to a lack of customer service. When too many patrons walk out without making purchases, or when the number of browsers falls steadily, something is drastically wrong. Pricing may be a problem, especially if discount competition has opened nearby. Some promotion might be needed to provide an image of savings, and remember to flaunt such store services as special ordering, mailing, gift wrapping, and wide selection.

EXPANSION

Expansion can cause a bookstore to fail. The three most common reasons for this are people-related:

(1) the owner/manager's time is split between the units, and none receives adequate supervisory attention;

(2) the owner/manager spends all of his or her time at the new store and the staff of the old store has not been properly trained to take on managerial duties and responsibilities; and

(3) customers have come to expect the bookseller to be there in person to share his or her knowledge and experience. Some patrons go elsewhere when that personal service and attention are not available.

Premature expansion sometimes uses up available capital and cash flow that is still needed to make the original bookstore a viable business. In addition, a new branch too close to the original store may be taking a profitable segment of the clientele away. The decrease in sales volume might result in the original store's inability to cover fixed expenses.

SUMMARY

In short, the bookseller who recognizes changes in market demographics, clientele, business and residential districts, merchandise demand, staff productivity, or the store's financial condition gains an advantage, especially when budgeting inventory and operating expenses. Energetic, inquisitive management should wonder periodically where people will be shopping in two to five years, which title categories are growing or developing, and what the new construction nearby, or lack of it, will mean in terms of clientele. Failure to heed such signs can prove fatal if sales have already started to decline. Keeping abreast of the latest developments allows the bookseller to grow a healthy business.

9

Thoughts on the Future of Bookselling

I am the supreme optimist about bookselling, and always have been. Perhaps that is why my fifty years of bookselling have been both a vocation and an avocation.

The future for books and bookselling is great, in spite of dire predictions flowing from many in the book world. Plato still lives, and so do Shakespeare, Dickens, Balzac, Hemingway, Robert Frost, and thousands of other great writers and thinkers from our past. Because of the book, ideas, achievements, and all of history are passed on and rediscovered. And as long as there are books, there will be bookstores.

The recent explosion of audiovisual machines and other communications products has not dented the steady increase in book reading and book buying. There is even evidence that some of these products have enhanced the use of books. I do not detect a substitute in the foreseeable future.

The following is a collection of thoughts that enforce my optimism about the future for booksellers:

(1) Books entertain, give pleasure, educate, offer quiet and solitude, and can influence people to act and proceed in the right directions.

(2) More and more people are giving books as gifts.

(3) The number of people who are highly educated is growing steadily.

(4) The carriage trade image and snob appeal of bookstores continues to diminish. Almost anyone feels comfortable walking into a bookshop now. Where there used to be a small percentage of people buying a lot of books occasionally, there are now lots of people buying books. Booksellers should now appeal to the top 85% or more of the potential market, rather than just the most affluent.

(5) Children are reading at an earlier age today. I believe the great increase in the number of children's bookshops is evidence of this. Reading habits developed at an early age will create more and more readers and book buyers for the future.

(6) The growth of tie-ins with radio, TV, movie, and other programming creates more demand for related books.

(7) The increasing cost of many other kinds of entertainment makes books and reading a more attractive leisure-time activity.

(8) The availability and sale of books in more kinds of retail outlets and mail-order firms helps sell more books and promotes reading. Many people buy their first book in museums, national park stores, kitchen, garden, sports departments and stores, travel shops, and even swap meets. The promotion of books anywhere is ultimately good for all bookstores.

(9) The growth of specialized bookshops should motivate publishers to seek out and issue more specifically crafted books. This should attract more first-time book buyers.

(10) The relatively large segment of the population that does not currently frequent bookstores, yet reads magazines and newspapers and borrows books from libraries, provides a market waiting to be tapped through novel ways.

(11) Booksellers are becoming better retail store operators, more adept at buying, selling, and merchandising books. This is especially true of independent booksellers, so many of whom have learned the importance of controlling their inventories and

operating expenses. I like to think that much of this change has resulted from the ABA Booksellers Schools and other Association teachings. The average merchant has become more professional in the trade.

(12) I believe that many publishers waste advertising and promotion money by hyping too much in some areas and not enough in others. There is room for them to become more skillful in the use of the various media, and to spread their budgets into more markets and on more titles. I have hopes that more effort will be made to promote more general and specialized nonfiction titles by reducing spending on many bestsellers.

(13) There will be breakthroughs on the literacy front. More and more organizations, private and public, are focusing on the intolerable statistics about illiteracy, and many programs have been started to improve the situation. It is to be hoped that federal and state governments will pay a larger part in funding projects that will encourage more people to learn to read. As literacy grows, the use of books will grow, and so will the buying of books by many who presently have no interest.

(14) With public libraries suffering from inadequate funds to keep their collections up to date, many people will be buying books that are not available in libraries.

(15) Much literary criticism is written for a scholarly, "intellectual" audience, seemingly ignoring the other 75% of the reading public. Testimonials of sports, movie, and other famous figures help sell many products. Why not books?

(16) Bookstore chains and independent merchants are opening bookshops in hundreds of cities and towns that do not have well-stocked stores. Good new stores do create new book readers and buyers.

(17) More people are discovering the joy of reading, and the benefits of reading for knowledge. The growth of book sales in nonconventional retail outlets, such as airports and hotels, and the great interest shown in them by passersby creates impulse buyers, many of whom become repeat buyers.

(18) Although publishers have improved their trade terms in recent years, I believe the best is yet to come. Some publishers will recognize the importance of bookstores as their main outlets, and will help increase profit with more favorable discount schedules and buying terms. The growth of competition in other communication products could help this come about. I believe the resurgence and new success of the independent bookseller will prove to publishers that they can sell their books.

(19) I believe there will be technological advances in book manufacturing, especially hardbounds, that will lower the cost of producing them. This will allow a reduction in list prices, or at least a moderation of increases. This should help increase the sale of books.

(20) I foresee some federal or state "fair trade" legislation in the next few years. When it is recognized that many small businesses are closing because of price competition and large store buying advantages, some action will be taken—for example, minimum markups above cost rather than maintaining list price sales. This would help the economics of bookselling and motivate expansion of current bookshops and the opening of more new stores.

Admittedly, some wishful thinking has crept into these thoughts. But I really believe that most of them will come to pass and make future bookselling even grander and more profitable for more booksellers.

Appendix

Case Examples

Every day booksellers must make decisions and resolve problems that can have a lasting impact on their business. The following case examples are designed to help you avoid potential pitfalls and manage your bookstore more effectively.

Find the Shoppers, and You'll Find the Business

Go with the big merchants, if you can afford it, is one of my axioms. When word got out that we were opening a branch in a nearby city, many publisher's reps questioned our decision. They insisted that the established bookshops had all the book business that was available in town. But we believed that the big department stores involved in building the new regional mall had done their homework and must be confident that they would attract the shoppers. Our advantage would be that we would have the greatest selection. In the first year, we doubled the sales in the market, and the bookstore continued to grow. The other bookshops also remained in business for years.

*They Can't Buy Your Books
If They Can't Find Your Store*

I was really astounded when I saw the way in which a new community shopping center was being constructed. It had about 20 store spaces in a line, all facing the highly traveled main street in town, and had good parking. That was fine. But two walkways led to the rear, each containing about 5 spaces on either side. The two lanes led to another dozen spaces at the back. I felt that it was a very poor layout, with most of the walkway stores having little or no visibility and the rear stores having none at all. Even though it was a very high-income area, I predicted problems. The front line spaces were leased fairly quickly, but only about a third of the walkway and rear spaces were occupied in the first two years. In the third year, the center was taken over by another company; the new owners tore down all the rear sections and most of the walkway construction and are now reconstructing and reshaping the center, ensuring that future stores will have good to excellent visibility to potential customers. Visibility is an important factor in locating your store.

What Should You Look for When Buying Someone's Inventory of Books?

A woman called me about a small bookshop she was about to buy in her hometown. She had made an oral agreement to pay $50,000, and she had until the end of the month to decide. I questioned her about what her money was buying and discovered that: $40,000 was for the inventory at 40% of retail; the store had rarely taken the time to return overstocks; no new titles had been ordered for more than two months; and many books seemed in used condition. I also found that sales had declined steadily over the past year and that the store would have to close if not sold soon. The value of the stock on the balance sheet was carried at full cost of $60,000. In addition, the prospective buyer had not evaluated the inventory book by book, nor had she negotiated the asking price. I concluded that the inventory was probably not worth more than 20% of list price, about $20,000, and recommended that she not buy the store. But if she decided at the end of the month that she still wanted it, she should offer only $30,000 for the business, and tell the owner why. She got it, saving $20,000.

Before Signing the Lease, Get a Second Opinion

A former librarian planned to open a children's bookshop in a large strip shopping center. Because I knew the area well, she asked me to look over the lease that she was ready to sign. When we discussed her sales projections, I discovered that her figures were at least double my estimate of what the market and location would produce in the first year. After analyzing the rental terms in the lease, it was obvious that the space was not affordable if my estimates were correct, and was even very questionable based on her higher projections. I suggested that she not accept the lease contract because:

(a) the base rent in itself would equal more than 20% of my estimate of first year's sales;

(b) additional listed occupancy charges for common area maintenance, mandatory merchants' association fees, and annual basic rent increase in line with the Consumer Price Index could add 3% to 6% of sales in space costs. Even if sales doubled within five years, total rent would remain more than 10% of sales, placing a handicap on other expenses and potential profit.

Lease terms should always be analyzed, word by word, by an experienced person.

Listen to Customers When Stocking Your Store

At the time I moved from a great bookstore in Cambridge to another great bookstore in Hollywood, I thought I knew everything about stocking a bookstore. But one factor I had not adequately explored in my former location was why people were asking for titles that I did not stock. I quickly discovered in my new position that the inventory included a great many titles that I had not previously considered as basic stock, and even some that were unfamiliar to me. How did this store find these titles? The answer was simple: The owner trained his

people to question customers about books they were looking for
that were not in stock, especially when it was a second request.
In that way, the buyer knew to stock a certain book on mother-
hood, and one on divorce, and a particular law dictionary, and
a textbook on nursing, and a book on middle east religion, and
so forth. Most were not for college courses but were specially
recommended for one reason or another. Some were stocked
and sold in very large quantities, and few were available in other
stores.

Anticipate Average Sales Per Title and Stock Accordingly

Our average branch stores stocked between 10,000 and
25,000 titles during a year, as do most growing independent
bookshops. I used to take delight in throwing a merchandising
question at some staff member: "What do you think is the
average number of copies sold during the year of all titles
stocked?" The response was usually 20, 15, or 10. I would then
say to reduce the number and would hear 8, 7, or 6. When I told
them that the answer was probably between 2 and 4, they were
shocked. The employees tended to think in terms of bestsellers,
familiar titles, and big displays. They did not consider all those
titles stocked in ones and twos, and sold in twos, ones, and zeros.
That type of thinking is what often misleads even experienced
buyers. It's important to limit large-quantity purchases to bestsellers and other proven titles.

Don't Be Misled by False Indicators of Success

I was working with the owner of a large bookstore, and we
were discussing buying procedures. I was told that the
Religion/Philosophy category had produced the biggest sales
for the past two years. It also had the largest nonfiction display
in the store. Having gone through the same experience in

another general bookshop recently, I had to question the owner about it: "Have you totaled the returns of overstock from this section?" I asked. The answer was no. I suspected that four or five titles constituted most of the sales, and it did add up to a great deal of money. What was happening was that the buyer was influenced by the quarterly category reports showing Religion/Philosophy to be one of the top two in sales. He kept adding new titles, taking up more space and investment than was warranted. The inventory should not be expanded solely on the basis of total dollar sales, because bookselling is mainly a title business.

Why You Should Deal with Complaints Quickly

I did not mind answering customer complaints that came in the mail. That was a lot easier than trying to satisfy an angry patron, face to face, and convince him or her that the store did not usually foul up. One day I received a customer's diatribe in the mail, blasting the store and all our people for sending the wrong book and card to a friend in the hospital in another city. After fretting about it for a couple of hours, I called the customer to apologize and admit our mistake. I offered to call a bookstore in the other city and have them deliver the correct book by messenger that day, all at our expense. I also said I would mail a note of explanation to her friend. Our accusing customer, who had vowed never to shop with us again, was so grateful for our efforts that she became one of the store's most loyal customers.

Make Every Inch of Space Count

I was involved in the bidding for the inventory of a failed bookstore. Thinking about the reason for the business' downfall, one factor stood out. Although the store was in a much-used community shopping center in a good market, there was poor use of space. Rent was being paid on almost twice the amount of selling space. Nonselling space included an office, a storeroom, a shipping/receiving area, and an employees' lounge—all for a store doing about $200,000 a year. We decided to lease the space and operate a bookstore there, because we were convinced that using the space more efficiently with more selling and display area could double the volume in two years. We did.

Be a Tightwad When Buying Supplies

Two booksellers opened their stores in the same city at about the same time in the 1970s. One owner grew his bookshop to a large volume in five years, but the other attained only 60% the volume in the same time. The first merchant was a penny-pincher, while the other was a waster. Such traits were easy to detect after knowing the booksellers for a while, talking shop, and comparing merchandising and operating expenses. For example, the prosperous bookseller never bought a box in which to return overstocks to publishers. The less successful owner packed all his returns in newly purchased cartons. There is "fat" that may be eliminated in almost all expenses, if they are analyzed.

Growing Sales Volume Does Not Guarantee Growing Profit

A bookstore opened in 1984 with a first year's sales plan of $200,000. The owner used most of his personal savings plus a loan from the bank. Actual sales for the first year came to $225,000, and the first three months of the second year showed a 45% increase, predicting a $325,000 volume for the full year. The happy bookseller started to have grand ideas, adding lots of inventory and staff, including an assistant buyer. He also purchased a computer and system for stock control. He felt fortunate to have an empty store next door, which he leased, doubling the size of the bookstore (doubling the rent, too). He expanded in the middle of the second year, and that year sales did reach $325,000. But, in spite of the added space and stock, the third year sales were only $375,000, a 15% increase. Inventory costs and operating expenses had expanded too fast, and there was no operating profit those first three years after a meager compensation draw by the owner. The bookshop is now in its fourth year, and sales are increasing at about an 8% to 10% rate, while the owner tries to reduce inventory and control expenses. It won't be until the sixth year of operation that this bookseller will be able to draw an acceptable compensation and profit. He was fortunate that the bank increased his loan and extended his payments so he could bring the business back to an even keel and profit potential. Too soon and too large expansions have doomed many retail stores.

There's No "Easy Money" in Stocking School Texts in General Bookstores

One year, three branch store managers called me in early September and said they had ordered some course books at the request of local instructors. I heard the same story in each case about unhappy teachers who came into the store crying that the campus store never seemed to have enough copies of books for their classes, or failed to get them on time. The teachers promised to send all their students to our bookstore if we stocked the titles. Our excited managers saw a chance for added sales and jumped at the opportunity. But the managers were not experienced with student habits, and sure enough, the students went to the campus store or other college supplier first and bought their books, leaving our branch stores stuck with almost all of their copies.

Keep Written Records of Discipline and Performance

It is becoming more and more difficult to discharge employees without getting in trouble with labor boards. Dismissed workers increasingly are claiming that they were let go without legal cause. At one time, only very large companies were hit by lawsuits for wrongful discharge, but now even very small businesses are facing these actions. A five-year employee of a small bookshop took her firing to the labor department, claiming she was discharged without cause, and that she had never been told by the owner of problems with her work. She claimed her age was the reason. The merchant claimed that she was let go because she was often late for work and took extended lunch hours. The owner, however, had no written work schedules or warning notice to back up his claims. The worker said that such occurrences were infrequent, and no more often than any other employee. She won the case and was awarded two-months' back pay.

Are Your Employees Productive?

Two large bookstores in adjacent towns were owned by friends. One was very profitable, while the owner of the other struggled to make the business break even. After a bad year, the owner of the less prosperous operation requested help from his friend, who had obviously become very affluent from his bookstore business. In comparing figures, the two shops showed similar sales histories, inventory and sidelines selections, and the like. But in assessing staffs, it became immediately obvious why the bookstore had problems—almost twice the work hours were scheduled each week in the struggling operation. Work functions were too divided among specialists, who were not performing in all areas of the store. Poor productivity was the result.

Here's One Way to Catch Shoplifters

A person well known in the community visited his local bookshop often. He was friendly with the employees and always made a point of greeting one or two of them while browsing, sometimes asking a question about a book. But an alert staff member became suspicious of his behavior and also realized that although this customer spent most of his time looking at hardbound books, his only purchases were occasional low-priced paperbacks. After a discussion with the owner, it was decided to watch the customer from an unseen vantage point on his next visit. Sure enough, he was seen slipping a $15 book under his jacket and was apprehended as he was leaving the shop. Questioning brought an admission that he took this one book. A threat to get the police involved produced another confession; he had pilfered many more books, which he had at home, and he agreed to return them. While most customers are honest, all bookstore people should realize that sometimes shoppers do steal books, and that it has a damaging effect on store business and profit.

Controlling Register Voids and No-Sales

One day, as I was doing my usual monitoring of the selling action, I noticed a purchase being made by a customer. The salesperson had rung up a no-sale, and the receipt was put in the bag with the books. Curious, I caught up with the customer at the front door and said that the clerk had made a mistake; would it be all right if I took back the receipt, since the payment was correct for her $19.90 purchase? I called the department manager and salesperson to my office to examine the full contents of the cash drawer. We also obtained a total of all transactions thus far that day. A count showed a 10¢ shortage, and not a $19.90 overage. It seemed obvious that $20 had been pocketed. We told the whole story to that salesperson, who then acknowledged taking the $20 without further questioning and even before he was accused.

If a Cash Register Could Talk

A bookstore had large shortages two years in a row, although it had an experienced manager in charge. No ready answer was found for the abnormal shrinkages. A veteran security person was called in by the owner without anyone else's knowledge. One possible clue was found in the cash register tape with detail numbers for each opening of the register. Analysis showed gaps in receipt numbers between the last ring at night and the first ring the next day. Further investigation and interrogation of the person who closed the store on both nights brought an admission that he had closed out the register an hour early each night and taken the money on sales made during that time. He then put in a new tape for the next day, forgetting about receipt numbers. Register tapes can be an important factor in money control.

Don't Let Your Employees Succumb to Temptation

A bookstore owner had a feeling that the assistant manager was pocketing register money. The employee had worked in the store for five years, but there had been signs over the last year of a change in attitude. Also, he was always volunteering to work nights and weekends, times when the owner was not generally present. Checking the records for a recent period, the owner found that sales totals when the assistant closed the store were less than usual, and that there were also more no-sale and void receipts rung up. The owner decided to make a test. She balanced out the register as usual at 6 o'clock one night and left the bookshop. She then gave a friend $50 to go to the store and buy an unabridged dictionary. The friend made the purchase and brought the book back without a receipt, which was not offered to him by the assistant. The owner returned to the store 20 minutes later and checked the register tape and money. She found a voided receipt for the full cost of the dictionary and another ring-up on the register tape for exactly $20 less. And the register balanced. The assistant admitted that he had pocketed the $20 under-ring. Management must be aware that some employees are susceptible to the desire for a little of "all that money that comes into the store register," and take steps to make it as difficult as possible.

Are Your Shipments Coming Up Short?

A large-volume bookstore had a full-time and a part-time shipper/receiver. The full timer was fast and methodical and seemed efficient. During his second year on the job, the store owner began to realize that there was an extraordinarily large number of shortages on shipments from publishers, as reported by the work room. Although the store received credits for these shortages, the owner felt that the discrepancies were too far out of line with industry averages. No publisher complained of the chargebacks, because the receiver spread the shortages around among the hundreds of resources used by the bookshop. The owner decided to make a test, with the cooperation of a friendly local publishing person. When the paperwork was received in the office, sure enough, there was a one-copy shortage noted. A simple interrogation produced an admission that the receiver took home most of the books that he claimed were missing in the received packages.

Do You Know Where Your Money Goes?

A $500,000 volume bookstore attained good profit results, but lately the owner could not draw much of the profit because there never seemed to be enough cash on hand. The Profit and Loss Statement showed reasonable gross margin and operating expenses, and the inventory figures indicated good turnover. Analyzing the situation, we discovered that gross margin was really an assumed figure, because no record of markdowns was made and no physical inventory had been taken over the past two years. Therefore, there was a reasonable assumption that gross margin, and hence net profit, were overstated. When physical inventory was taken, it was found to total about $20,000 less than the bookkeeping figure, a 4% shortage at retail. Because it was unlikely that it was all markdown and ordinary shortage, we felt there was a security problem. After carrying out a detailed inspection of accounting records, we felt that strong questioning of the bookkeeper was in order. Discussions with the bookkeeper revealed the existence of a dummy accounts payable record, with altered payables and purchases. Periodic payments to a fictitious publisher had been made by checks amounting to approximately $10,000 over the course of a year, and then mailed to a friend by the bookkeeper. This owner should have known to pay closer attention to the paperwork before signing anything.

If You Don't Ask, You Won't Get

An aggressive, independent bookstore owner alerted me years ago to one way she earned and received non-cash advertising co-op rebates. One day she complained vigorously to a publisher's rep about how difficult it was for her bookstore to obtain advertising rebates and about the recordkeeping involved. At the time, there was a good display of this publisher's bestselling book in the window. The rep satisfied the merchant by taking three copies of the book from his car and giving them to her. The retail value amounted to about ten percent of the bookshop's previous year's purchases at cost. The incident prompted the merchant to ask other publishers for window-display advertising allowances, sending them pictures of the windows and suggesting they send display or reading copies. She did receive some from time to time. Remember, any kind of rebate is profit.